Sight Word Tales ™

Teaching Guide

Easy Lessons, Practice Pages & Reproducible Versions of All 25 Storybooks

SCHOLASTIC

New York ○ Toronto ○ London ○ Auckland ○ Sydney
New Delhi ○ Mexico City ○ Hong Kong ○ Buenos Aires

Teaching Resources

Teaching guide written by Pamela Chanko
Cover design by Maria Lilja
Interior design by Grafica, Inc.
ISBN: 0-545-01643-6 / ISBN-13: 978-0-545-01643-8

Contents

The Mini-Books

Introduction

Welcome to *Sight Word Tales*—the fun, motivating way to learn sight words! These delightful stories teach the top 100 Dolch words—long recognized as the most important words to learn in order to form a basis for reading success—all in an appealing, engaging context. What are sight words? Reading research shows that 50 to 75 percent of text is made up of common, repeated words. Knowing these words by sight—that is, being able to recognize them immediately and without thought—greatly increases reading fluency and comprehension. The Sight Word Tales program includes the 100 most frequently repeated words children are likely to encounter in their reading material.

So why teach sight words? Take a look at these sentences:

We like to read. Some books are very good.

It's likely that you were able to take in the meaning of each sentence as a whole, simply because words such as *we, like, to, some, are, very,* and *good* are so familiar that they barely require a glance to convey meaning. As mature readers, we may take this lightning-fast process for granted. But to a child who is just beginning to read, these sentences look quite different. Children who need to analyze each letter in order to sound out the words *we, like,* and *to* may have already forgotten their meaning by the time they get to the word *read.* In order to comprehend the sentence, they would then need to go back to the beginning and read it a second time. Now imagine going on to the next sentence and going through the same process all over again. How likely is it that you would remember the first sentence once you'd deciphered the second?

It's clear that learning sight words—also called high-frequency words—is essential to reading success. The ability to recognize a word immediately is called *automaticity,* and it is particularly important in English because many of the most commonly repeated words do not follow regular phonetic rules. Of course, phonics is an indispensable part of any balanced literacy program, but words such as *come, would,* and *what* cannot be reliably decoded and therefore require memorization.

Research has shown that merely relying on context and exposure to language, hoping children will simply "pick up" sight words at their own pace, is a losing strategy. Sight words must be taught directly. On the other hand, studying and memorizing lists of words is unlikely to engage children. That's where *Sight Word Tales* comes in! With this program, you get the best of both worlds—an opportunity to provide direct, targeted instruction while addressing meaning, context, and children's need for fun, all at the same time. So open up a *Sight Word Tale* and open the door to reading success!

Using the Program

With the storybooks and this easy-to-use teaching guide, you've got all the tools you need to implement the *Sight Word Tales* program in your classroom.

Storybooks

In the handy storage box, you'll find 25 bright, full-color storybooks perfect for read-alouds as well as interactive reading. Each Sight Word Tale introduces four sight words; you'll find the target words printed on the front cover for easy access. What's more, these target words fit naturally into each and every tale. There are no forced or awkward plot lines; just fun, engaging stories that children will want to read again and again! From a little girl's desire for a pet in *Can We Get a Pet?* to a monkey's classroom visit in *Please Stop Monkeying Around!*, the storybooks are sure to hold children's interest as they build essential early reading skills. For tips on how to use the books, see pages 6 to 7 of this guide.

Mini-Books

This teaching guide contains a reproducible version of all 25 storybooks, so it's easy for every child to have a complete set of his or her own. The mini-books are great for independent reading, center work, and home-school connections. For more mini-book tips, see pages 8 to 9.

Book-by-Book Reproducibles

Research shows that children retain word knowledge far better when they work with a word in a variety of ways. In order to internalize a word, children need to hear the sounds in the spoken word, use manipulatives to build the word, and write the word. On pages 19 to 43, you'll find reproducible activity sheets that provide children with each of these important experiences. Each storybook has a corresponding reproducible that teaches the same four featured words, inviting children to say each word aloud to hear the sounds, write the word, and build the word using cut-out letters.

Activities and Games

In addition to reading and writing, children need to play with words in order to make them a permanent part of their vocabulary. On pages 13 to 18 of this guide, you'll find lots of suggestions for quick and easy activities designed to reinforce sight-word knowledge.

Assessment

As children add to their sight vocabularies through the storybooks, mini-books, reproducibles, and activities, you'll want to keep tabs on their progress. On pages 10 to 11 you'll find assessment tips and easy-to-use assessment sheets to help you track the development of every child in your class.

Using the Storybooks

The *Sight Word Tales* storybooks introduce sight vocabulary in such an engaging way that they're sure to become a favorite part of your classroom's read-aloud library. Here are a few tips for helping children get the most out of each book:

Before Reading

◎ Display the cover and read the title of the book aloud. Invite children to use the title and cover illustration to make predictions about the story. For instance, when introducing *Come to the Zany Zoo*, you might ask: What is unusual about the animal on the cover? What other kinds of animals do you think you might see at a zany zoo? If you like, make a quick list of children's predictions on the board or chart paper. Then return to your list after reading the story to see how many of the children's predictions were correct.

◎ Introduce the four sight words shown on the cover of the book. Read each word aloud as you point to it. Explain to children that these are sight words—words they can learn to recognize just by looking at them, without having to sound them out. Tell children that in this story, they will see these four words again and again.

◎ Next, turn the book over and read aloud the blurb on the back cover. Ask children if they see any of the words they read on the front cover. Point out the words in bold type, and explain that these four words are printed in bold throughout the story, too. Skim through the book, having children point out a few of the bold words. Read the words aloud, inviting children to echo-read after you.

During Reading

◎ On your first reading of the storybook, read straight through just for pleasure. Invite children to look at the illustrations as they become engaged in the story and language.

◎ The next time you read the story, encourage children to be on the lookout for the four words printed on the cover—the words in bold type. Read the words aloud before you begin reading the story, and invite children to signal whenever they hear or see one of the words. Children might participate by raising their hands or giving a "thumbs-up" each time one of the words appears.

◎ On a subsequent reading, pause to read aloud the blurb that appears on the first page of the story. Point out that children have already practiced looking for the words in the text—their new job is to find them in the pictures. Encourage children to spot the sight words in the speech bubbles as well as within the illustrations. For instance, on page 3 of *Let's Make Soup Together*, children will see the sight word *take* printed on a poster on the wall. On page 4 of *All Puffins Just Love Muffins*, children can find the sight word *just* on the cover of a cookbook.

◎ Once you've read the book several times, invite children to read along on words they know, particularly the targeted sight words. When you come to a target word, take a pause as you point to it, giving children time to chime in.

◎ As children become more and more familiar with the storybook, they'll be excited to take on increasing amounts of text. You can invite children to participate in a whole-class choral reading, have volunteers each read one page at a time, or even have pairs do a partner reading for the group.

After Reading

◎ Invite children to make comments and ask questions related to the story. You can spark ideas with questions such as: What was your favorite illustration? What part of the story surprised you? Who was your favorite character? and so on.

◎ Use the review on page 14 to gauge children's grasp of the four sight words. Point to each word at random, inviting children to read it aloud. Ask children who recognize the word what clues they used. For children who are having trouble, provide hints that can help them remember the word, such as the shape of the letters, the beginning or ending sound, and so on.

◎ The sentence fill-ins on page 15 help children use each of the sight words in context. Read aloud the words in the word box, and then read aloud each sentence, asking children to choose the word that fits best in the blank. When children become more familiar with this activity, you can ask them to make up their own cloze sentences. Try creating fill-ins as a group. For instance, for the sight word *can*, ask children to name something they can do. Then construct a sentence around their responses, for example: We _____ tie our shoes. Write the cloze sentence on chart paper and invite a volunteer to fill in the missing word.

◎ To celebrate children's learning, have fun with the cheers on page 16. Before you begin, help children practice spelling each sight word. Point to each letter in the words in the upper right corner, asking children to call out the letter's name. Once you've spelled out each word a few times, invite children to join in chanting each cheer.

◎ You can delve even deeper into each sight word by playing quick games that focus on word construction. For instance, when learning the word *well*, invite children to name words that rhyme (*bell, tell, fell*). When learning the word *stop*, encourage children to come up with words that begin with the same blend (*stick, stamp, stay*). You can do similar activities to focus on final consonants and vowel sounds.

Using the Mini-Books

With the reproducible mini-books, each child can assemble a personal library of Sight Word Tales. The mini-books not only strengthen children's reading and word recognition skills but also provide a great tool for forging home-school connections. Follow these tips to get the most out of the Sight Word Tales mini-books both inside and outside the classroom.

◎ **Read along with the storybook.** After reading a Sight Word Tale aloud a few times, give children copies of the mini-book pages and help them assemble their own copy of the book. As you read the storybook again, invite children to follow along in their own copies, tracking the print as they go. You can also ask children to participate with mini challenges, for instance: Point to the word *go* each time it appears on this page; hold up your fingers to show how many times the word *see* appears on this page; and so on.

◎ **Set up a learning center.** As you teach each group of sight words, you can create a center for independent work in which children can get additional practice with the words. Make multiple copies of the mini-book you are working with, and place them in the center along with copies of the book's practice pages (see pages 19 to 43). After reading the book and completing the activity sheet, encourage children to work with and build the words in additional creative ways by providing magnetic letters, letter tiles, letter stencils, and so on.

◎ **Build a personal library.** Gather a clean, empty shoebox for each child (you might ask families to bring them in from home). Provide children with construction paper, glue, stickers, gift wrap, crayons, and markers, and invite children to decorate the outside of their boxes. You can have children write their name on a cut sentence strip and attach it to the box as a label. Then let children use the boxes to store their collection of Sight Word Tales mini-books.

◎ **Create a listening center.** Make recordings of yourself reading the stories aloud, and place the mini-books in the center so that children can follow along with your reading. To add a professional touch to the recordings, you might even ring a bell to signal that it's time for children to turn the page.

◎ **Involve family members.** After working with the storybooks at school, use the mini-books to involve family members in their children's learning. The more children have exposure to, and repetition with, the targeted words, the more quickly they will become part of children's automatic sight vocabulary. Make a copy of the mini-book for children to bring home, and create a badge with the pattern at right. This creates a warm invitation for parents and caregivers to share the book with their child. You can also suggest that family members engage in additional activities, such as hunting for the target words in newspapers, magazines, labels, and environmental print.

Making the Mini-Books

1. Make double-sided copies of the mini-book pages. (You should have two double-sided copies for each one.)

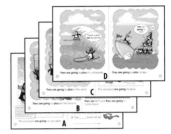

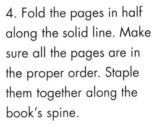

2. Cut the pages in half along the dashed line.

3. Position the pages so that the lettered spreads (A, B, C, D) are faceup. Place the B spread on top of the A spread. Then, place the C and D spreads on top of those in sequence.

4. Fold the pages in half along the solid line. Make sure all the pages are in the proper order. Staple them together along the book's spine.

Making the Badge

Make one copy of the badge for each child. Write the four sight words from the mini-book on the lines. Invite children to color the badge, if they like. Then punch a hole at the top and string with yarn to make a necklace that children can wear home.

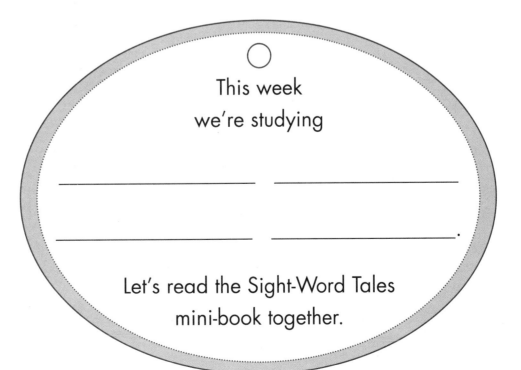

This week we're studying

_____   _____

_____   _____.

Let's read the Sight-Word Tales mini-book together.

Assessment

As you use the Sight Word Tales storybooks and mini-books in your classroom, it's likely that you'll see improvement in children's sight word skills, including word recognition, reading, spelling, and ability to use the words in context. As you move through the program, the goal is for children's sight word vocabulary to grow cumulatively; that is, recognizing four words after working with the first book, eight words after working with the second book, and so on. For this reason, you'll want to keep track of how well children are retaining the words they've learned so far.

For a quick and easy assessment technique, create flash cards by writing the four target words from the book on index cards. Next, copy the assessment sheet at right and write the four words in the first column. Then run off a class set, and write each child's name at the top. The sheet allows for individual assessment on four dates; write the date of your first assessment in the first Date column. Then shuffle the flash cards and hold up one at a time at random, having the child read the word. If the child reads the word correctly, make a check mark next to that word on the sheet. If the child reads the word incorrectly, reteach it and test him/her at a later date. As children's sight vocabulary grows, the assessment sheet grows along with it! As you work with more books, simply create additional flash cards. By the end of the program, children will have studied 100 words.

In addition to recognizing and reading the sight words, you'll want to assess how well children can spell the words, along with their ability to use the words in a complete sentence. To perform a spelling assessment, simply call out one word at a time from your flash-card deck and give children time to write each word on a lined sheet of paper. To assess children's ability to use the words in context, have them make up an oral or written sentence using each word.

The rubric below can be used as a general guideline for assessing children's overall progress. As is the case with all learning skills, note that children's sight vocabulary grows along a continuum; there are no hard-and-fast categories or rules. In addition, children may be stronger in some areas than in others. Use all your assessments in tandem to gauge which skills to focus on with each child.

Sight Word Rubric	Beginning	Developing	Accomplished	Advanced
Assessment Score	70% correct or below	80% correct	90% correct	100% correct
Sight Word Skills: • Recognition • Reading • Spelling • Ability to use in a complete sentence	Needs help with all four skills	Needs help with two or more skills	Needs help with one skill	Can accomplish all four skills with no help

Sight-Word Assessment: Words 1–50

Student's Name: _____

Sight Word	Date/✔	Date/✔	Date/✔	Sight Word	Date/✔	Date/✔	Date/✔
1. can				26. will			
2. we				27. it			
3. get				28. up			
4. no				29. was			
5. come				30. not			
6. to				31. a			
7. the				32. with			
8. see				33. don't			
9. this				34. be			
10. is				35. there			
11. too				36. under			
12. for				37. does			
13. look				38. want			
14. at				39. yes			
15. that				40. say			
16. go				41. in			
17. my				42. one			
18. and				43. by			
19. I				44. jump			
20. like				45. how			
21. he				46. do			
22. put				47. make			
23. on				48. laugh			
24. of				49. shall			
25. she				50. bring			

Sight-Word Assessment: Words 51–100

Student's Name: _____

Sight Word	Date/✔	Date/✔	Date/✔	Sight Word	Date/✔	Date/✔	Date/✔
51. him				76. buy			
52. or				77. who			
53. are				78. would			
54. going				79. these			
55. they				80. funny			
56. play				81. try			
57. some				82. again			
58. very				83. fall			
59. good				84. down			
60. but				85. take			
61. have				86. together			
62. you				87. then			
63. ask				88. around			
64. her				89. please			
65. help				90. stop			
66. them				91. if			
67. all				92. must			
68. just				93. little			
69. today				94. has			
70. so				95. find			
71. as				96. found			
72. well				97. once			
73. many				98. upon			
74. which				99. far			
75. kind				100. away			

Sight Word Games and Activities

Use these quick and easy ideas to give children hands-on experiences with the sight words they learn from Sight Word Tales.

Sight Word Wall

Designate a bulletin board or wall space at children's eye level for a sight word wall. As children learn sight words from the books, simply write them on index cards and add them to the wall. You can use your growing word wall for a variety of activities and games.

◎ **I Spy a Sight Word** Choose a "secret" word from the wall and give children clues to guess its identity, for instance: I spy a sight word that begins with the letter *p*. This word rhymes with *day*. It has four letters. Continue giving clues until a child guesses the word (*play*). That child then chooses a new word and gives clues for the group to guess.

◎ **Sight Word Spotlight** Dim the classroom lights and give one child a flashlight. Call out a word from the wall and challenge the child to shine the light on that word. Continue until each child has had a turn. Alternatively, you can divide the class into two teams and give one child from each team a flashlight. The first child to shine the light on the correct word earns his or her team a point.

◎ **Word Chain** Call out a word from the wall, such as *can*. Then challenge a child to find a word that begins with the last letter, such as *not*. The next child then finds a word that begins with the last letter of the previous word, such as *then*. Continue until the word chain is broken (that is, there are no words that begin with the last letter of the previous word). Then call out a new word and start a new chain.

Transition Time Sight Words

You can squeeze in sight word practice at any time of day with these quick ideas.

◎ **Lining Up** Write sight words on index cards, creating two matching sets. Tape one set of cards to the floor where children usually line up. Place the other set in a box. Each time children need to line up, have them choose a card from the box. Then challenge children to line up by standing on the spot with the matching word. Alternatively, you can give each child a word card and challenge children to line up by putting themselves in alphabetical order.

◎ **Find a Partner** Write pairs of matching sight words on index cards and place the cards in a bag or box. When children need to find partners for an activity, have each child pick a card. Children who picked the same card can find each other and work together.

◎ **Snack Time** Create sight word place mats by writing target words on sheets of construction paper and laminating them or covering them with clear contact paper. Write matching words on index cards. Before snack time, place the mats on the table and give each child a random word card. Invite children to find their place at the table by finding the matching word on a place mat.

◎ **Cleaning Up** When it's time to clean up, call out sight words one at a time. Have children spell out the word, count the number of letters, and then put away the same number of items.

◎ **Time to Go** When it's time to pack up, avoid the cubby crush by giving each child an index card with a sight word. Invite small groups to go to their cubbies by calling out different categories, for instance: everyone whose word contains the letter *p*; everyone who has a five-letter word; everyone whose word begins with a *t*; and so on.

Touchy-Feely Spelling

Tactile learners will benefit from sensory writing experiences. You can squirt shaving cream on a cookie sheet and have children write sight words in the cream using a finger. If they make a mistake, they can "erase" by smoothing the cream over with their palm. You can also fill a plastic tub with damp sand and have children spell words using a dowel. As a third option, fill a zip-close sandwich bag halfway with tinted hair gel. Write sight words on large index cards and have children place the gel bag on top of a card. Children can use their finger to trace the letters in the gel.

Sight Word Scavenger Hunt

Give each child a list of target words, a stack of old magazines, a sheet of construction paper, scissors, and glue. Then have children hunt through the magazines for the words on their list. Each time they find a word, they can cut it out and glue it on the paper. When finished, children will have a sight word collage, most likely filled with lots of different fonts and colors.

Silly Sentence of the Day

Write target sight words on small slips of paper and place them in a bag. Each day, have a different volunteer choose three to five words from the bag (depending on children's skill level). Then have the whole class work together to write a silly sentence containing all the words. For instance, if a child draws the words *want, jump,* and *funny,* the sentence might be: *We want to jump like funny frogs.* Write the sentence on a sheet of chart paper, using a different color marker for the target words. You can add a new sentence to your chart each day.

Hop 'n' Type

This activity is fun for all children, and especially good for kinesthetic learners. On an old bed sheet or shower curtain liner, use a permanent marker to write letters in squares to make a giant QWERTY computer keyboard. (You can include only the letter keys, leaving out the numerals and punctuation marks.) Use masking tape to attach the keyboard securely to the floor. Then let children take off their shoes and have them line up behind the keyboard. As each child steps up to the keyboard, call out a random sight word and have the child hop on the appropriate "keys" to spell out the word! Continue until each child has had a turn.

Sight Word Scramble

Use alphabet letter cards to play this fun game. Choose a "secret" sight word and gather the appropriate letters to spell the word. Then call a number of children up front (the same number of children as letters in the word). Huddle up with children and whisper the secret word, giving each child a letter card. Then have children stand in a row facing the group, and hold their letter cards in front of them in mixed up order. Children in the audience then take turns asking one child at a time to move to a different spot; for instance: Keisha, go stand between Andres and Jake. Then the next child gets to move a letter. Children can move only one letter on their turn. Have children continue to rearrange the letter-holders until they're standing in the correct order. Once the word is unscrambled, choose a new sight word and a new team of letter-holders.

Sight Word Tic Tac Toe

Draw a tic tac toe grid on the board and divide the class into two teams, X's and O's. Fill each space in the grid with a sight word. The game is played just like regular tic tac toe, with members of each team choosing a space to cover. In order to mark the space with an X or an O, the team member must read the word in that space correctly. The team that gets three X's or O's in a row wins the game.

Shake-a-Word

To prepare this game, get a clean, empty egg carton and small self-stick labels. Write sight words on 12 labels and stick one in each cup of the carton. Then place a number cube inside the carton. In groups of two to four, have children play the game as follows. The first player closes the carton and shakes it. He or she then opens up the carton and notes what number is facing up on the cube. The child then removes the cube and reads the sight word that's printed in the cup in which the cube landed. If the child reads the word correctly, he or she earns the number of points shown on the cube. Then it is the next player's turn. Children can play for a set number of rounds or as time permits.

Sight Word Baseball

Gather in an open area and create four "bases" by placing beanbags or books on the floor to make a mini baseball diamond. Write on index cards any sight words you'd like to reinforce and divide the class into two teams. You can play the game similarly to regular baseball. Have one team go up to "bat" by lining up behind home plate. "Pitch" a word to the first player by holding up an index card. If the player gets a "hit" by reading the word correctly, he or she moves to first base and it is the next hitter's turn. For each word a hitter reads correctly, each child on the diamond moves forward one base. When a child gets to home base, a point is earned for that team. Each time a child misses a word, the team gets an "out." Three outs, and it's the next team's turn! You can continue to play the game for a set number of "innings."

Sentence-Builder Hangman

This version of "hangman" reinforces both spelling and how words are used in context. Choose a "mystery" sight word and build a sentence around it, writing blanks for the letters of the target word. For instance, for the word *around*, you might write: The dog chased the cat __ __ __ __ __ __ the yard. Just like regular hangman, children guess one letter at a time. If the letter appears in the word, write it in the appropriate space. If not, add one body part to the "hangman." Children try to solve the word before the hangman's body is complete!

Sight Word Blotto

This game adds an element of chance, so even a beginning reader can get the most points. In advance, write sight words you'd like to reinforce on index cards. For about every ten cards, create a "blotto" card by writing Blotto! in big red letters. Set an amount of time to play (about 10 to 15 minutes). Then place all the cards in a bag or box and have children take turns coming up to pick a card. If the child can read the word, he or she keeps the card. If not, it goes back in the box. Children will begin to accumulate cards, but any child who draws a "blotto" card must place all of his or her cards back in the box and start from scratch! When time is up, children can count their cards to see who has the most.

Sight Word Bingo

Write 20 to 25 sight words on the board, and write the same words on separate index cards. Then give each child a bingo grid with 16 squares. To create their game boards, children can choose any 16 words from the board and write one in each square. Give children counters or dried beans to use as markers. To play, place the index cards in a paper bag and pull out one at a time at random. If children have the word on their board, they can cover it with a marker. The first child to get four in a row (vertically, horizontally, or diagonally) calls out Bingo! Then have children clear their boards and play another round.

Go Fish

Create a deck of cards by writing 26 sight words on separate index cards. Write each word twice on each card, and cut the cards in half to make a deck of 52 cards. Children can play the game in groups of three to six. Each player gets five cards, and the remaining cards are placed facedown in the middle. The first player chooses a word from his or her hand and asks another player for the matching word card. If the player has the card, he or she hands it over. If not, that player says, "Go fish," and the first player picks the top card from the middle deck. If the drawn card makes a pair, the player places the pair on the table. If not, the player keeps the card and it is the next player's turn. Play continues until one player runs out of cards or the middle deck is used up.

can	we
get	no

Use with *Can We Get a Pet?*

Name _____

Write each word.

can _____   we _____

get _____   no _____

Cut out the letters. Use them to build each word.

we

no

can

get

t a e o c w n n e g

Name _____

Write each word.

come

___ ___ ___ ___

the

___ ___ ___ ___

to

___ ___ ___ ___

see

___ ___ ___ ___

Cut out the letters. Use them to build each word.

come

[ ][ ][ ][ ]

the

[ ][ ][ ]

to

[ ][ ]

see

[ ][ ][ ]

e s h t e m c o o t e e

Use with *Come to the Zany Zoo*

come to
the see

| this | is |
| too | for |

Name _____

Use with *A House for Mouse*

Write each word.

this _____

_ _ _ _ _ _ _ _ _ _ _ _ _ _ _ _ _ _

is _____

_ _ _ _ _ _ _ _ _ _ _ _ _ _ _ _ _ _

too _____

_ _ _ _ _ _ _ _ _ _ _ _ _ _ _ _ _ _

for _____

Cut out the letters. Use them to build each word.

this

is

too

for

o s t o t h s o i i i f r

Name _____

Write each word.

look _____

that _____

at _____

go _____

Cut out the letters. Use them to build each word.

that

look

at

go

t o t a o l a o h k g t

Name _____

Use with *My Dragon and I*

Write each word.

my _____

I _____

and _____

like _____

Cut out the letters. Use them to build each word.

my

I

and

like

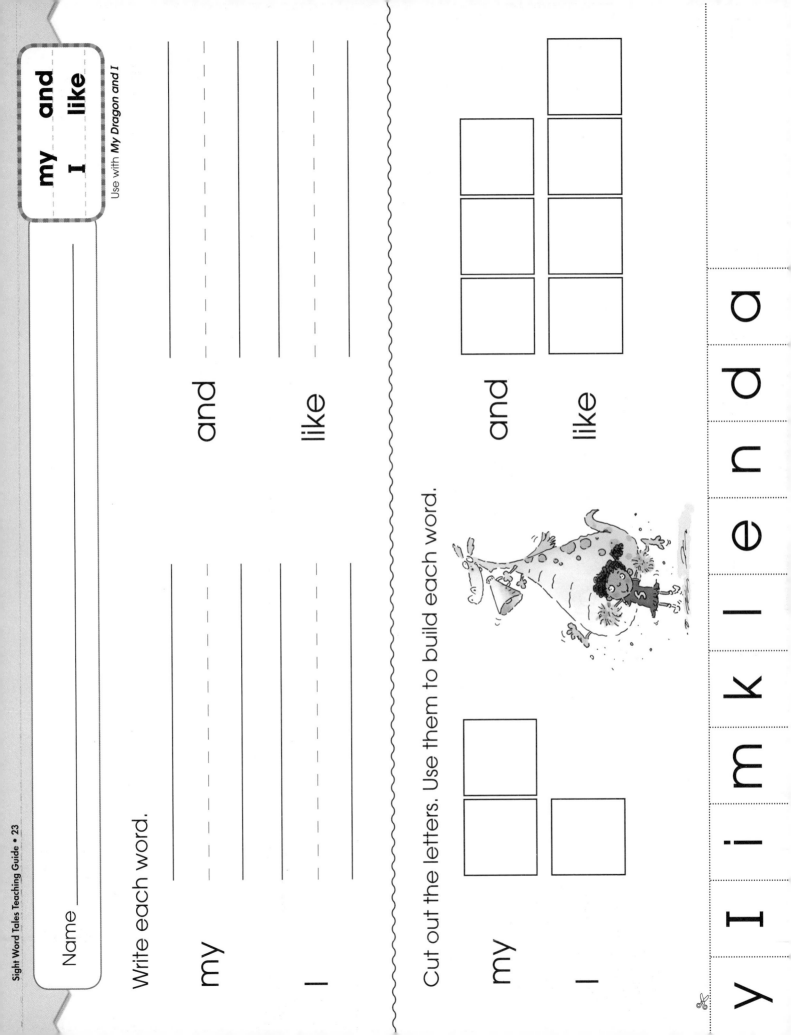

y I i m k l e n d a

Write each word.

on _ _ _ _ _ _ _ _ _ _ _

he _ _ _ _ _ _ _ _ _ _ _

put _ _ _ _ _ _ _ _ _ _ _

of _ _ _ _ _ _ _ _ _ _ _

Cut out the letters. Use them to build each word.

on

he

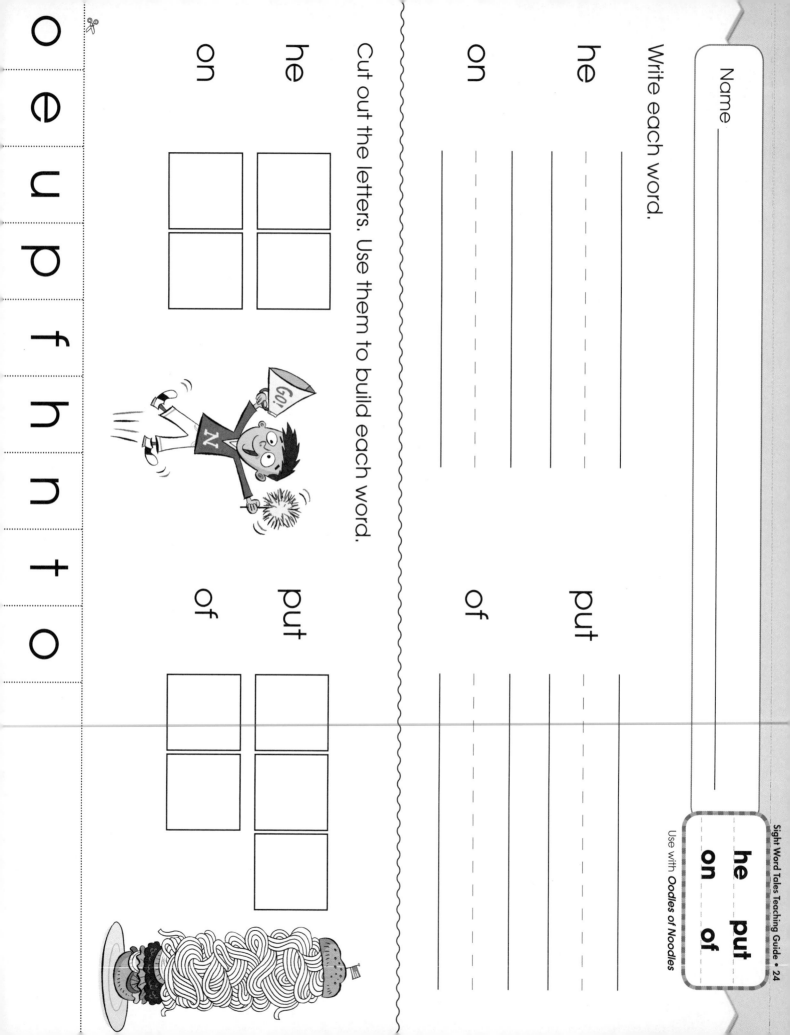

put

of

o e u p f h n t o

Name _____

she will
it up

Use with *The Fix-It-Up Fairy*

Write each word.

she _____

will _____

it _____

up _____

Cut out the letters. Use them to build each word.

she

will

it

up

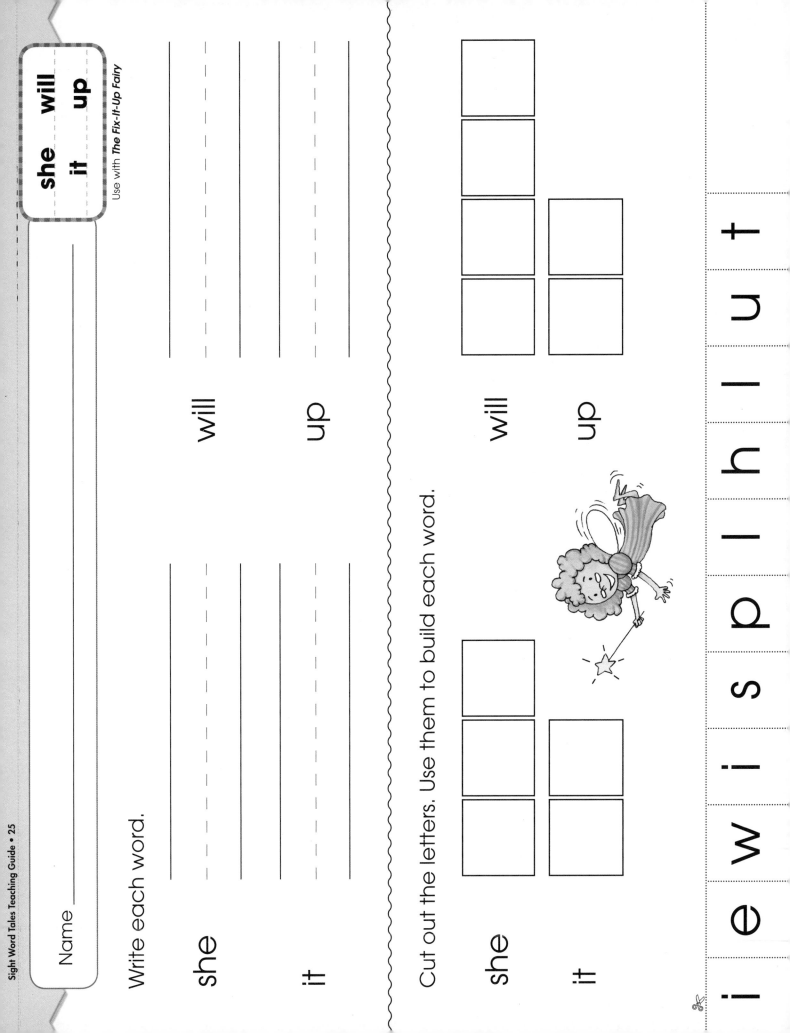

i e w i s p l l h l u t

i

Write each word.

was _____

a _____

not _____

with _____

Cut out the letters. Use them to build each word.

was

a

not

with

w n w h i a a o s t t

Use with **A Book With a Pig**

was   not
a   with

don't	there
be	**under**

Use with *Don't Be Afraid, Monster*

Name _____

Write each word.

don't _ _ _ _ _ _ _ _ _ _ _ _ _ _

there _ _ _ _ _ _ _ _ _ _ _ _ _ _

be _ _ _ _ _ _ _ _ _ _ _ _ _ _

under _ _ _ _ _ _ _ _ _ _ _ _ _ _

Cut out the letters. Use them to build each word.

don't

there

be

under

d h r b o t t n e u r d e

e e n e u r d e

Write each word.

does _ _ _ _ _ _ _ _ _ _ _ _ _ _ _ _ _

yes _ _ _ _ _ _ _ _ _ _ _ _ _ _ _ _ _

want _ _ _ _ _ _ _ _ _ _ _ _ _ _ _ _ _

say _ _ _ _ _ _ _ _ _ _ _ _ _ _ _ _ _

Cut out the letters. Use them to build each word.

does

yes

want

say

w u n s e d a t o y y s e a s

Use with *Does Polly Want a Cracker?*

does want
yes say

Name _____

Use with *One by One*

Write each word.

one _____ _____

in _____

jump _____ _____

by _____

~~~~~~~~~~~~~~~~

Cut out the letters. Use them to build each word.

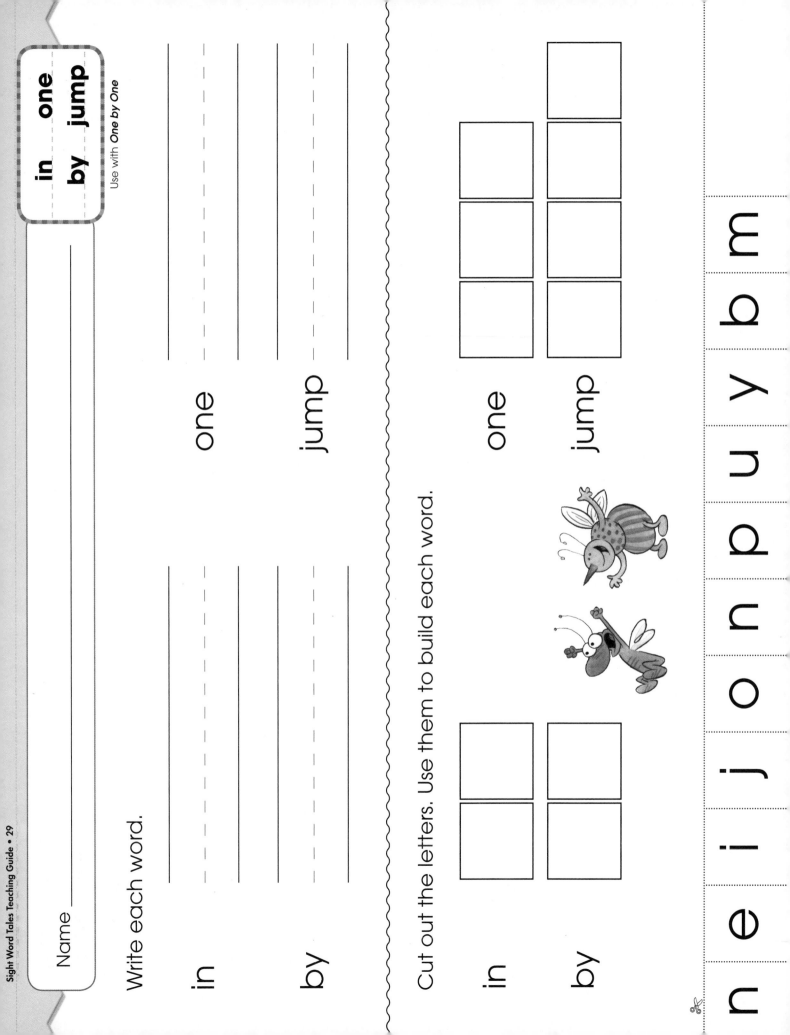

one

jump

in

by

n e i j o n p u d u y b m

Write each word.

how _ _ _ _ _ _ _ _   do _ _ _ _ _ _ _

make _ _ _ _ _ _ _   laugh _ _ _ _ _ _ _

Cut out the letters. Use them to build each word.

how

make

do

laugh

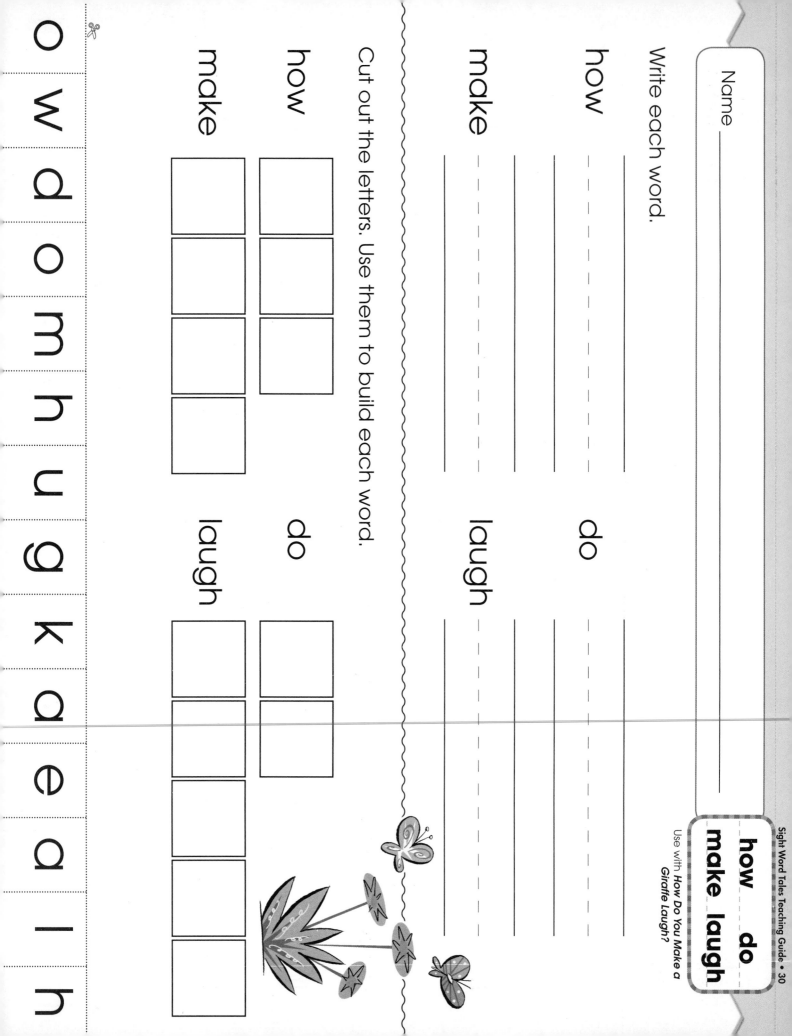

o w d o m h u g k a e a l h

Use with *How Do You Make a Giraffe Laugh?*

**how   do
make   laugh**

Name _____

| shall | him |
| bring | or |

Use with *What Shall I Bring the King?*

Write each word.

shall _____

him _____

bring _____

or _____

- -

Cut out the letters. Use them to build each word.

shall [   ][   ][   ][   ][   ]

him [   ][   ][   ]

bring [   ][   ][   ][   ][   ]

or [   ][   ]

l   l   a   h   h   i   o   b   r   i   m   s   r   g

Name _____

are going
they play

Use with *The Penguins Are Going on Vacation*

Write each word.

are _____   going _____

they _____   play _____

Cut out the letters. Use them to build each word.

are   going

they   play

e a n y y i e r g h t o g l p a

some very
good but

Use with **Some Dogs Are**
Very Good

Name _____

Write each word.

_____

very

_____

but

some

_____

good

_____

Cut out the letters. Use them to build each word.

very

but

some

good

b d v o e m g u o o o t y r s e

Write each word.

have

_____

_____

ask

_____

_____

you

_____

_____

her

_____

_____

Cut out the letters. Use them to build each word.

have

ask

you

her

v u o h e s e a r y h a

k

Use with **Have You
Seen Jellybean?**

**have   you
ask   her**

help	them
all	just

Name _____

Use with *All Puffins Just Love Muffins*

Write each word.

help _ _ _ _ _ _ _ _

them _ _ _ _ _ _ _ _

all _ _ _ _ _ _ _ _

just _ _ _ _ _ _ _ _

Cut out the letters. Use them to build each word.

help

them

all

just

t p h m e u l l l e a h l j j t s

✂

Write each word.

today —

as —

so —

well —

Cut out the letters. Use them to build each word.

today

as

so

well

o a e a t s y l s o d w

a a s y o d w l

Use with *Today Is So Boring*

today   so
as   well

| many | which |
| kind | buy |

Name _____

Use with *So Many Kinds of Shoes!*

Write each word.

many _____

which _____

kind _____

buy _____

Cut out the letters. Use them to build each word.

many

which

kind

buy

n m w y i h y d h a i c k u b n

Write each word.

who ___ ___ ___ ___ ___ ___   would

these ___ ___ ___ ___ ___ ___   funny

- - - - - - - - - - - - - - - - - - - -

Cut out the letters. Use them to build each word.

who [ ][ ][ ]   would [ ][ ][ ][ ][ ]

these [ ][ ][ ][ ][ ]   funny [ ][ ][ ][ ][ ]

u d t l o e f n s e o w h u n y w h

Use with *Who Would
Buy These Clothes?*

**who   would
these   funny**

try	again
fall	down

Name _____

Use with *Try Again, Hen!*

Write each word.

try _____

_____

again _____

_____

fall _____

_____

down _____

_____

Cut out the letters. Use them to build each word.

try

again

fall

down

g w t n a a y d a y l n i o f l r

Write each word.

take _____

then _____

together _____

around _____

Cut out the letters. Use them to build each word.

take

together

around

then

t t h u a h g e o e t e r o r e d t a k n n

Use with *Let's Make Soup Together*

take together
then around

Name _____

please   if
stop   must

Use with *Please Stop*
Monkeying Around!

Write each word.

please

_____
_____

if

_____
_____

stop

_____
_____

must

_____
_____

Cut out the letters. Use them to build each word.

please

if

stop

must

l f p s u t i a e o p p e s t m s

Name _____

Write each word.

little _____

find _____

has

found _____

- -

Cut out the letters. Use them to build each word.

little ☐ ☐ ☐ ☐ ☐ ☐

find ☐ ☐ ☐ ☐

found ☐ ☐ ☐ ☐ ☐

has ☐ ☐ ☐

i i a n d u f s a h l n t f o e t l

Use with *Little Bo-Peep's Lost-and-Found Sheep*

little has
find found

Name

Write each word.

once

upon

get

away

Cut out the letters. Use them to build each word.

once

upon

far

away

o f a n o r n a c u e w p y a

Celebrate the new sight words you learned by saying these four short cheers.

C-a-n! Give a yell!
What do these three letters spell?
A sight word that we all know well —
Can, can, can!

W-e! Give a yell!
What do these two letters spell?
A sight word that we all know well —
We, we, we!

G-e-t! Give a yell!
What do these three letters spell?
A sight word that we all know well —
Get, get, get!

N-o! Give a yell!
What do these two letters spell?
A sight word that we all know well —
No, no, no!

16

Sight Word Review

can	we
get	no

Do you know the four sight words in this book? Read aloud the word on each bone.

we   get
no
      we
get
      can
no
      can

Sight Word Tales

can	we
get	no

Can We Get a Pet?

by Maria Fleming
illustrated by Amy Wummer

SCHOLASTIC

No!

Can we?

Can we get a rat?
No!

3

Sight Words

Sight words are words that you see again and again when you read. This book is filled with the sight words **can**, **we**, **get**, and **no**. Look for them in the text. Check the pictures, too!

Can we get a snake?
No!

2

A

Can we get a monkey?
No!

4

B

Sight Word Fill-ins

can	we
get	no

Listen to the sentences. Then choose a sight word from the box to fill in each blank.

Word Box   can   we   get   no

1 After dinner, _____ can have ice cream!

2 Did you _____ wet in the rain?

3 There are _____ cookies left.

4 She _____ hit a ball.

5 Let's _____ a book from the library.

6 I have _____ pets.

7 Yes, _____ are going to the party.

8 I _____ ride a bike!

Answers: 1. we 2. get 3. no 4. can 5. get 6. no 7. we 8. can

15

Can we get a dog?
Okay.
Okay? HOORAY!

13

Can we get a skunk?
No!

Can we get a bat?
No!

Can we get a goat?
No!

Can we get a goose?
No!

Can we get a raccoon?
No!

6

C

Can we get a frog?
No!

11

Can we get a beaver?
No!

8

D

Can we get a moose?
No!

9

Sight Word Cheers

Celebrate the new sight words you learned by saying these four short cheers.

C-o-m-e! Give a yell!
What do these four letters spell?
A sight word that we all know well —
Come, come, come!

T-o! Give a yell!
What do these two letters spell?
A sight word that we all know well —
To, to, to!

T-h-e! Give a yell!
What do these three letters spell?
A sight word that we all know well —
The, the, the!

S-e-e! Give a yell!
What do these three letters spell?
A sight word that we all know well —
See, see, see!

16

Sight Word Review

Do you know the four sight words in this book? Read aloud the word on each shoe.

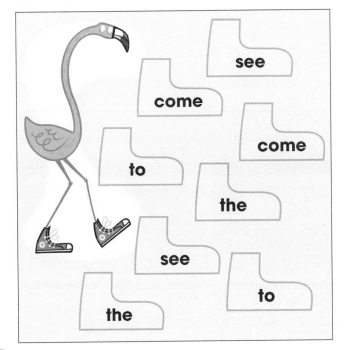

see
come
come
to
the
see
to
the

14

Sight Word Tales

Come to the Zany Zoo

by Jane Quinn
illustrated by Jim Paillot

SCHOLASTIC

It is fun **to** twirl!

Come to the zany zoo!
Come see the hippo in a tutu!

3

Welcome to the ZaNY ZOO come oN iN!

Sight Words

Sight words are words that you see again and again when you read. This book is filled with the sight words **come, to, the,** and **see.** Look for them in the text. Check the pictures, too!

Come to the zany zoo!
Come see the polka-dot kangaroo!

2

A

Sight Word Fill-ins

Listen to the sentences. Then choose a sight word from the box to fill in each blank.

Word Box	**come**	**to**	**the**	**see**

1. Can I _____ with you?

2. He will _____ his aunt next week.

3. The teacher told us not _____ run.

4. She cannot _____ over today.

5. I will be a fairy in _____ play.

6. Did you _____ that big bug?

7. We love _____ have picnics.

8. Let's go on _____ swings.

Answers: 1. come 2. see 3. to 4. come 5. the 6. see 7. to 8. the

15

I **see** I need **to** tie my shoe.

Come to the zany zoo!
Come see the flamingo in one pink shoe!

4

B

Glad you could **come.**

Hi! Nice **to see** you.

Come to the zany zoo!
Come see the animals.
They want **to see** you!

13

Come to the zany zoo!
Come see the lion with a fancy hairdo!

The boat is going **to** sink!

Come to the zany zoo!
Come see the elephant in a canoe!

Moo!

Come to the zany zoo!
Come see the tiger who only says, "Moo!"

Come to the zany zoo!
Come see the leopard play a kazoo!

Come to the zany zoo!
Come see the panda play peek-a-boo!

6

C

I love **to** celebrate **the** 4th of July!

Come to the zany zoo!
Come see the zebra who is red, white, and blue!

11

See my picture!

Come to the zany zoo!
Come see the bear make things with glue!

8

D

The answer is four.

Come to the zany zoo!
Come see the alligator add two plus two!

9

Celebrate the four new sight words you learned by saying these short cheers.

T-h-i-s! Give a yell!
What do these four letters spell?
A sight word that we all know well —
This, this, this!

I-s! Give a yell!
What do these two letters spell?
A sight word that we all know well —
Is, is, is!

T-o-o! Give a yell!
What do these three letters spell?
A sight word that we all know well —
Too, too, too!

F-o-r! Give a yell!
What do these three letters spell?
A sight word that we all know well —
For, for, for!

16

Sight Word Review

| this | is |
| too | for |

Do you know the four sight words in this book? Read aloud the word on each brick.

this

too   for   is

for   too

is   this

Sight Word Tales

| this | is |
| too | for |

A House for Mouse

by Maria Fleming
illustrated by Tammie Lyon

◼ SCHOLASTIC

Too small!

This house **is too** small.

3

Too big!

Sight Words
Sight words are words that you see again and again when you read. This book is filled with the sight words **this**, **is**, **too**, and **for**. Look for them in the text. Check the pictures, too!

Mouse needs a house.
This house **is too** big **for** Mouse.

2

A

Listen to the sentences. Then choose a sight word from the box to fill in each blank.

| Word Box | **this** | **is** | **too** | **for** |

1. We had pizza _____ lunch.

2. My mom made me _____ hat.

3. I was _____ sick to go.

4. These books are _____ you.

5. My favorite snack _____ popcorn.

6. What is _____ mouse doing in my room?

7. He _____ my friend.

8. It was _____ cold to swim.

Answers: 1. for 2. this 3. too 4. for 5. is 6. this 7. is 8. too

15

Too round!

This house **is too** round **for** Mouse.

4

B

This is the house **for** me!

This house **is** just right!

13

This house **is too** wet **for** Mouse.

This house **is too** tall.

This house **is too** cold **for** Mouse.

This house **is too** hairy.

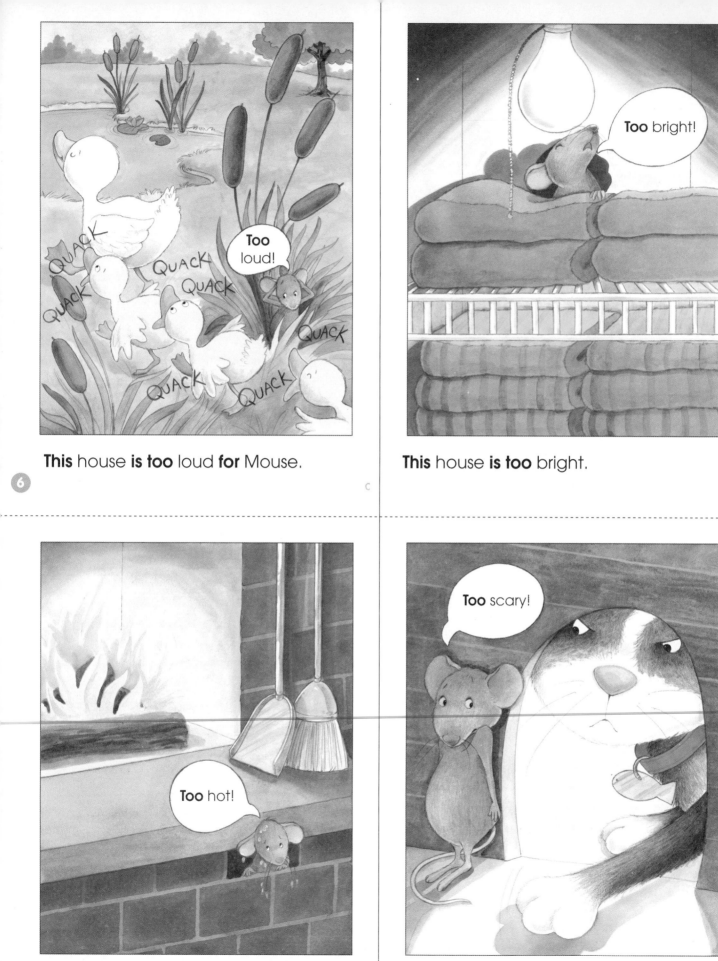

This house **is too** loud **for** Mouse.

6

C

This house **is too** bright.

11

This house **is too** hot **for** Mouse.

8

D

This house **is too** scary.

9

Sight Word Cheers

Celebrate the new sight words you learned by saying these four short cheers.

L-o-o-k! Give a yell!
What do these four letters spell?
A sight word that we all know well —
Look, look, look!

A-t! Give a yell!
What do these two letters spell?
A sight word that we all know well —
At, at, at!

T-h-a-t! Give a yell!
What do these four letters spell?
A sight word that we all know well —
That, that, that!

G-o! Give a yell!
What do these two letters spell?
A sight word that we all know well —
Go, go, go!

16

Look at That Cat!

by Maria Fleming
illustrated by Patrick Girouard

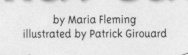

■ SCHOLASTIC

Sight Word Review

Do you know the four sight words in this book? Read aloud the word on each medal.

14

Go, cat, go!

Look at that cat throw!
Go, cat, **go!**

3

Look at that cat run!
Go, cat, **go**!

2

A

Sight Word Fill-ins

Listen to the sentences. Then choose a sight word from the box to fill in each blank.

Word Box	**look**	**at**	**that**	**go**

1 I left my book _____ home.

2 I _____ like my twin sister.

3 Did you _____ to the park?

4 He wants _____ dog.

5 You _____ sleepy today.

6 Let's _____ to the movies.

7 We saw a tiger _____ the zoo.

8 I do not like _____ hat.

Answers: 1. at 2. look 3. go 4. that 5. look 6. go 7. at 8. that

15

Look at that cat swim!
Go, cat, **go**!

4

B

Look at that cat sleep!
It was only a dream! Oh, cat!

13

Look at that cat kick!
Go, cat, **go**!

12

Look at that cat row!
Go, cat, **go**!

5

Look at that cat skate!
Go, cat, **go**!

10

Look at that cat ride!
Go, cat, **go**!

7

Look at that cat lift!
Go, cat, **go**!

6

C

Look at that cat leap!
Go, cat, **go**!

11

Look at that cat fly!
Go, cat, **go**!

8

D

Look at that cat slide!
Go, cat, **go**!

9

Sight Word Cheers

Celebrate the new sight words you learned by saying these four short cheers.

M-y! Give a yell!
What do these two letters spell?
A sight word that we all know well —
My, my, my!

A-n-d! Give a yell!
What do these three letters spell?
A sight word that we all know well —
And, and, and!

I! Give a yell!
What does this one letter spell?
A sight word that we all know well —
I, I, I!

L-i-k-e! Give a yell!
What do these four letters spell?
A sight word that we all know well —
Like, like, like!

16

Sight Word Review

my	and
I	like

Do you know the four sight words in this book? Read aloud the word on each puddle.

my

I

and

like

I

my

like

and

14

My Dragon and I

by Maria Fleming
illustrated by Mike Gordon

SCHOLASTIC

I like sliding!

My dragon **and I like** to slide.

3

I like swinging!

Sight Words

Sight words are words that you see again and again when you read. This book is filled with the sight words **my**, **and**, **I**, and **like**. Look for them in the text. Check the pictures, too!

My dragon **and I like** to swing.

2

A

Sight Word Fill-ins

Listen to the sentences. Then choose a sight word from the box to fill in each blank.

Word Box	**my**	**and**	**I**	**like**

1. _____ have a cold.

2. We _____ to play games.

3. That is _____ pencil.

4. He had a peanut butter _____ jelly sandwich.

5. Do you _____ this book?

6. _____ won the race!

7. She has a brother _____ a sister.

8. Oh no, _____ tooth fell out!

Answers: 1. I 2. like 3. my 4. and 5. like 6. I 7. and 8. my

15

I like hopping!

My dragon **and I like** to hop.

4

B

I like my best friend!

My dragon is **my** best friend.

13

My dragon **and I like** to paint.

My dragon **and I like** to hide.

My dragon **and I like** to read.

My dragon **and I like** to splash.

My dragon **and I like** to climb.

6

My dragon **and I like** to pretend.

11

My dragon **and I like** to dig.

8

My dragon **and I like** to crash.

9

Sight Word Cheers

Celebrate the new sight words you learned by saying these four short cheers.

H-e! Give a yell!
What do these two letters spell?
A sight word that we all know well —
He, he, he!

P-u-t! Give a yell!
What do these three letters spell?
A sight word that we all know well —
Put, put, put!

O-n! Give a yell!
What do these two letters spell?
A sight word that we all know well —
On, on, on!

O-f! Give a yell!
What do these two letters spell?
A sight word that we all know well —
Of, of, of!

16

Sight Word Review

he put
on of

Do you know the four sight words in this book? Read aloud the word on each plate.

of

put

he

put

on

of

on

he

14

Sight Word Tales

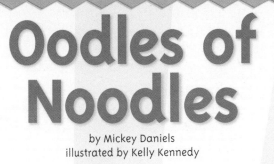

Oodles of Noodles

by Mickey Daniels
illustrated by Kelly Kennedy

SCHOLASTIC

He put noodles **on** waffles.
Oodles **of** noodles!

3

Noodles on celery. Yum!

Sight Words

Sight words are words that you see again and again when you read. This book is filled with the sight words **he**, **put**, **on**, and **of**. Look for them in the text. Check the pictures, too!

There once was a boy who **put** noodles **on** everything **he** ate. Oodles **of** noodles!

2

A

Sight Word Fill-ins

Listen to the sentences. Then choose a sight word from the box to fill in each blank.

Word Box	he	put	on	of

1. The cat is _____ the chair.

2. Where did you _____ your shoes?

3. She has a lot _____ freckles.

4. I like pepperoni _____ my pizza.

5. Is _____ your uncle?

6. We won three _____ the four games.

7. Please _____ away your toys.

8. Will _____ help us?

Answers: 1. on 2. put 3. of 4. on 5. he 6. of 7. put 8. he

15

You put noodles on peanut butter? Yuck!

He put noodles **on** sandwiches. Oodles **of** noodles!

4

B

Now **he puts** pickles **on** everything. Piles **of** pickles!

13

Then one day, **he** got tired **of** noodles.

He put noodles **on** hot dogs.
Oodles **of** noodles!

He put noodles **on** toast.
Oodles **of** noodles!

Oodles **of** noodles!

He put noodles on cake.

6

He even put noodles on noodles!
Oodles of noodles!

11

He put noodles on pizza.
Oodles of noodles!

8

He put noodles on ice cream.
Oodles of noodles!

9

Sight Word Cheers

Celebrate the new sight words you learned by saying these four short cheers.

S-h-e! Give a yell!
What do these three letters spell?
A sight word that we all know well —
She, she, she!

W-i-l-l! Give a yell!
What do these four letters spell?
A sight word that we all know well —
Will, will, will!

I-t! Give a yell!
What do these two letters spell?
A sight word that we all know well —
It, it, it!

U-p! Give a yell!
What do these two letters spell?
A sight word that we all know well —
Up, up, up!

16

The Fix-It-Up Fairy

by Catherine Bittner
illustrated by Richard Torrey

SCHOLASTIC

Sight Word Review

Do you know the four sight words in this book? Read aloud the word on each star.

she
it
will
up
she
up
it
will

14

Thank you, fix-**it-up** fairy!

She will fix **it** right **up**!

3

The fix-**it**-**up** fairy **will** fix anything!
Will she fix this doll?

2   A

Sight Word Fill-ins

she	will
it	up

Listen to the sentences. Then choose a sight word from the box to fill in each blank.

Word Box   she   will   it   up

1 The cat climbed _____ the tree.

2 The bus _____ come soon.

3 When is _____ going to the party?

4 We walked _____ a big hill.

5 Can you fix _____?

6 My dad _____ take us to school.

7 I think _____ might rain today.

8 Is _____ your big sister?

Answers: 1. up 2. will 3. she 4. up 5. it 6. will 7. it 8. she

15

Will she fix this bear?

4   B

Hooray for the fix-**it**-**up** fairy's friend!

13

Hooray for the fix-**it**-**up** fairy!

She will fix **it** right **up**! Oops!

Will she fix this wand?
She will. . . call a friend.

She will fix **it** right **up**! Oh, dear!

Will she fix this truck?

And her friend **will** fix **it** right **up**!

Will she fix this bike?

She will fix **it** right **up**! Yikes!

6

8

9

Celebrate the new sight words you learned by saying these four short cheers.

W-a-s! Give a yell!
What do these three letters spell?
A sight word that we all know well —
Was, was, was!

N-o-t! Give a yell!
What do these three letters spell?
A sight word that we all know well —
Not, not, not!

A! Give a yell!
What does this one letter spell?
A sight word that we all know well —
A, a, a!

W-i-t-h! Give a yell!
What do these four letters spell?
A sight word that we all know well —
With, with, with!

16

A Book With a Pig

by Maria Fleming
illustrated by Doug Jones

THE THREE LITTLE PIGS

SCHOLASTIC

Sight Word Review

was not
a with

Do you know the four sight words in this book? Read aloud the word on each cover.

with	not	a	was
not	was	with	a

14

It **was not** this book.

It **was not a** book **with a** glass slipper.

3

Was it this book?

I fell out of **a** book. Which book **was** it?

2

A

Sight Word Fill-ins

was	not
a	with

Listen to the sentences. Then choose a sight word from the box to fill in each blank.

Word Box	was	not	a	with

1 He did _____ want to go to the doctor.

2 My dog came _____ us to the park.

3 We read _____ book about bears.

4 Will you play _____ me?

5 She _____ sick yesterday.

6 Do _____ start the game yet.

7 The movie _____ very funny.

8 May I borrow _____ pencil?

Answers: 1. not 2. with 3. a 4. with 5. was 6. not 7. was 8. a

15

It was not this book.

It **was not a** book **with a** candy house.

4

B

But this is **a** very nice home!

13

Wow! That **was a** close call!
He **was not a** very nice wolf.

It **was not a** book **with a** giant.

It **WAS a** book **with** pigs...

It **was not a** book **with a** cookie.

It **was not a** book **with a** spider.

6

...and **a** wolf. RUN!!!

11

It **was not a** book **with a** troll.

8

It **was not a** book **with** bears.

9

Celebrate the new sight words you learned by saying these four short cheers.

D-o-n'-t! Give a yell!
What do these four letters spell?
A sight word that we all know well —
Don't, don't, don't!

B-e! Give a yell!
What do these two letters spell?
A sight word that we all know well —
Be, be, be!

T-h-e-r-e! Give a yell!
What do these five letters spell?
A sight word that we all know well —
There, there, there!

U-n-d-e-r! Give a yell!
What do these five letters spell?
A sight word that we all know well —
Under, under, under!

16

Don't Be Afraid, Monster

by Maria Fleming
illustrated by Mike Moran

SCHOLASTIC

Do you know the four sight words in this book? Read aloud the word on each pillow.

don't

there

under

be

there

don't

be

under

Clothes were **under there!**

There is nothing scary **under** the blanket.

Don't be afraid.

Sight Words

Sight words are words that you see again and again when you read. This book is filled with the sight words **don't**, **be**, **there**, and **under**. Look for them in the text. Check the pictures, too!

Don't be afraid, Monster.

2

A

Sight Word Fill-ins

don't be
there under

Listen to the sentences. Then choose a sight word from the box to fill in each blank.

Word Box **don't**   **be**   **there**   **under**

1 You can _____ so silly!

2 They _____ want to go.

3 The crayons are over _____.

4 My shoe was _____ the bed.

5 We _____ need our coats today.

6 Are _____ any more apples?

7 The ball rolled _____ the bush.

8 I have to _____ home by noon.

Answers: 1. be 2. don't 3. there 4. under 5. don't 6. there 7. under 8. be

15

Don't be afraid.

Don't be afraid, Monster.

4

B

Don't worry. I'll **be** right up here.

Z z z

Sweet dreams **under there**!

13

Time to go to sleep, Monster.

There is nothing scary **under** the desk.

Don't be afraid, Monster.

There is nothing scary **under** the coat.

Don't be afraid, Monster.

6

There is nothing scary **under** the bed.

11

Don't be afraid, Monster.

8

There is nothing scary **under** the towel.

9

Celebrate the new sight words you learned by saying these four short cheers.

D-o-e-s! Give a yell!
What do these four letters spell?
A sight word that we all know well —
Does, does, does!

W-a-n-t! Give a yell!
What do these four letters spell?
A sight word that we all know well —
Want, want, want!

Y-e-s! Give a yell!
What do these three letters spell?
A sight word that we all know well —
Yes, yes, yes!

S-a-y! Give a yell!
What do these three letters spell?
A sight word that we all know well —
Say, say, say!

16

Does Polly Want a Cracker?

by Jane Quinn
illustrated by Patrick Girouard

SCHOLASTIC

Sight Word Review

does want yes say

Do you know the four sight words in this book? Read aloud the word on each apple.

does want

want say yes

yes does say

Does it rhyme with cheese?

Yes, it does!

Say the magic word, Polly.
But Polly **does** not remember it.

14

3

Polly is hungry. **Does** Polly **want** a cracker?
Yes! Polly **does want** a cracker!

2

A

Does Polly **want** an apple?
Yes! Polly **does want** an apple!

4

B

Sight Word Fill-ins

does want
yes say

Listen to the sentences. Then choose a sight word from the box to fill in each blank.

Word Box   **does**   **want**   **yes**   **say**

1. Where _____ this bus go?
2. I _____ to read this book.
3. It is nice to _____ "please" and "thank you."
4. Is the answer _____ or *no*?
5. They _____ "hello" to us every morning.
6. She _____ not like rainy days.
7. We _____ to get a puppy.
8. I always say "_____" to ice cream.

Answers: 1. does 2. want 3. say 4. yes 5. say 6. does 7. want 8. yes

15

And Polly even remembers to **say**, "Thank you!"

13

"Polly **wants** an apple, PLEASE!
Polly **wants** a cracker, PLEASE!"

Say the magic word, Polly.
But Polly **does** not remember it.

"PLEASE!" Polly **says**.
Polly ***does*** remember it! She **does**!

Say the magic word, Polly.
But Polly **does** not remember it.

Does Polly **want** a sandwich?
Yes! Polly **does want** a sandwich!

6

Then she **says**, "Polly **wants** a sandwich,
PLEASE!"

11

Does Polly **want** a cupcake?
Yes! Polly **does want** a cupcake!

8

Say the magic word, Polly.
Polly thinks and thinks.

9

Sight Word Cheers

Celebrate the new sight words you learned by saying these four short cheers.

I-n! Give a yell!
What do these two letters spell?
A sight word that we all know well —
In, in, in!

O-n-e! Give a yell!
What do these three letters spell?
A sight word that we all know well —
One, one, one!

B-y! Give a yell!
What do these two letters spell?
A sight word that we all know well —
By, by, by!

J-u-m-p! Give a yell!
What do these four letters spell?
A sight word that we all know well —
Jump, jump, jump!

16

Sight Word Review

Do you know the four sight words in this book? Read aloud the word on each puddle.

jump
one
by
in
jump
by
one
in

14

Sight Word Tales

One by One

by Mickey Daniels
illustrated by Stacy Curtis

SCHOLASTIC

This **one** looks good.

I can't wait to **jump in**!

It's fun to **jump in** puddles!

The bugs are ready for some puddle-**jump** fun!

3

The rain passed **by**.
Now there's sun, sun, sun!

A

Sight Word Fill-ins

Listen to the sentences. Then choose a sight word from the box to fill in each blank.

Word Box	in	one	by	jump

1 Frogs can _____ very far.

2 I did it all _____ myself!

3 Fish live _____ the ocean.

4 He gave his dog _____ bone.

5 Put the pie _____ the oven to bake.

6 We had a picnic _____ the lake.

7 Do not _____ on the bed!

8 I have _____ sister.

Answers: 1. jump 2. by 3. in 4. one 5. in 6. by 7. jump 8. one

There goes ladybug!
Oh, what fun!

B

Hooray! A new puddle to **jump in**!

It's a bigger **one**!

It's a better **one**!

Until they find another **one**!

No **one**
wants to
play?

And that's the end
of their puddle-**jump** fun....

Nice **jump**!

The bugs **jump in**,
one by one.

There goes frog. Oh, no, no, no!
The bugs **jump** out and go, go, go —

The bugs **jump in**,
one by one.

There goes ant!
Oh, what fun!

C

all at once,
not **one by one**.

There goes caterpillar!
Oh, what fun!

D

The bugs **jump in**,
one by one.

Celebrate the new sight words you learned by saying these four short cheers.

H-o-w! Give a yell!
What do these three letters spell?
A sight word that we all know well —
How, how, how!

D-o! Give a yell!
What do these two letters spell?
A sight word that we all know well —
Do, do, do!

M-a-k-e! Give a yell!
What do these four letters spell?
A sight word that we all know well —
Make, make, make!

L-a-u-g-h! Give a yell!
What do these five letters spell?
A sight word that we all know well —
Laugh, laugh, laugh!

16

How Do You Make a Giraffe Laugh?

by Catherine Bittner
illustrated by Kelly Kennedy

■SCHOLASTIC

Sight Word Review

how do make laugh

Do you know the four sight words in this book? Read aloud the word on each balloon.

how

laugh

make

make

do

do

how

laugh

14

This will **make** you **laugh**!

How do you **make** a giraffe **laugh**?
Juggle some peas? No.

3

I know how to make you laugh!

Sight Words

Sight words are words that you see again and again when you read. This book is filled with the sight words **how**, **do**, **make**, and **laugh**. Look for them in the text. Check the pictures, too!

How do you **make** a giraffe **laugh**? Tickle his knees? No.

2

A

Sight Word Fill-ins

how   do
make laugh

Listen to the sentences. Then choose a sight word from the box to fill in each blank.

Word Box   **how**   **do**   **make**   **laugh**

1 Her dog can _____ tricks.

2 Please show us _____ to play the game.

3 That funny story made me _____.

4 Can you _____ a giraffe from clay?

5 I know _____ to ice-skate.

6 They _____ not live near us.

7 He will _____ soup for dinner.

8 I always _____ at clowns.

Answers: 1. do 2. how 3. laugh 4. make 5. how 6. do 7. make 8. laugh

15

How do you like it?

How do you **make** a giraffe **laugh**? **Make** balloon hats? No.

4

B

How exciting!

How did you know **how** to **make** him **laugh**?

I wish I knew **how** to **do** it!

I Can Make a Giraffe Laugh

Do it again!

Congratulations! You win the prize!

13

Look at that giraffe **laugh** and **laugh** and **laugh** till he cries!

How do you **make** a giraffe **laugh**? Dance with wombats? No.

Look **how** high I can jump!

BOING BOING BOING

How do you **make** a giraffe **laugh**? Act like a kangaroo? No.

How come this does not **make** you **laugh**?

How do you **make** a giraffe **laugh**? Wear an ape suit? No.

How do you **make** a giraffe **laugh**?
Balance some fruit? No.

6

How do you **make** a giraffe **laugh**?
Tell a joke or two? Yes!

11

How do you **make** a giraffe **laugh**?
Hang upside down? No.

8

How do you **make** a giraffe **laugh**?
Dress like a clown? No.

9

Celebrate the new sight words you learned by saying these four short cheers.

S-h-a-l-l! Give a yell!
What do these five letters spell?
A sight word that we all know well —
Shall, shall, shall!

B-r-i-n-g! Give a yell!
What do these five letters spell?
A sight word that we all know well —
Bring, bring, bring!

H-i-m! Give a yell!
What do these three letters spell?
A sight word that we all know well —
Him, him, him!

O-r! Give a yell!
What do these two letters spell?
A sight word that we all know well —
Or, or, or!

16

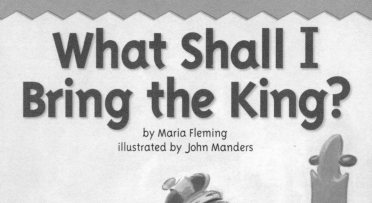

What Shall I Bring the King?

by Maria Fleming
illustrated by John Manders

■SCHOLASTIC

Sight Word Review

shall bring him or

Do you know the four sight words in this book? Read aloud the word on each gift box.

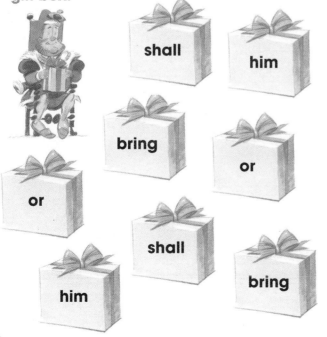

shall

him

bring

or

or

shall

him

bring

Shall I bring him a jump rope **or** a hula-hoop?

3

Sight Words

Sight words are words that you see again and again when you read. This book is filled with the sight words **shall**, **bring**, **him**, and **or**. Look for them in the text. Check the pictures, too!

Happy birthday to the king!
There's a party for **him**.
What **shall** I **bring**?

2

A

Listen to the sentences. Then choose a sight word from the box to fill in each blank.

Word Box	shall	bring	him	or

1 The teacher asked _____ a question.

2 I _____ not give up!

3 They will paint it blue _____ green.

4 We gave _____ a present.

5 She will _____ a gift to the party.

6 Do you have a cat _____ a dog?

7 Please _____ me that book.

8 What _____ we do today?

Answers: 1. him 2. shall 3. or 4. him 5. bring 6. or 7. bring 8. shall

15

You did not have to **bring** me a gift!

Shall I **bring him** a plane
that can loop-de-loop?

4

B

May your birthday **bring** you happiness.

May your birthday **bring** you sun.

May your birthday **bring** you friends.

May your birthday **bring** you fun.

No rubies **or** gold **or** diamonds,

Or fancy gifts **shall** do.

No, none of these can measure

How much we all love you!

I shall bring him a poem
that I write myself!

13

I know what I **shall bring** the king!

Shall I **bring him** a yo-yo
or a jack-in-the-box?

Or a flock of peacocks!

Or do kings have closets full of these things?

Shall I **bring him** pajamas
or slippers **or** socks?

6

C

Or a magical elf!

11

I **shall bring him** something
he does not have for sure.
I **shall bring him** a unicorn!

8

D

Or a dinosaur!

9

Sight Word Cheers

Celebrate the new sight words you learned by saying these four short cheers.

A-r-e! Give a yell!
What do these three letters spell?
A sight word that we all know well —
Are, are, are!

G-o-i-n-g! Give a yell!
What do these five letters spell?
A sight word that we all know well —
Going, going, going!

T-h-e-y! Give a yell!
What do these four letters spell?
A sight word that we all know well —
They, they, they!

P-l-a-y! Give a yell!
What do these four letters spell?
A sight word that we all know well —
Play, play, play!

16

Sight Word Tales

The Penguins Are Going on Vacation

by Catherine Bittner
illustrated by Doug Jones

SCHOLASTIC

Sight Word Review

Do you know the four sight words in this book? Read aloud the word on each pail.

going are they play

they play going are

14

They are going to play and have fun.

3

Top-left panel (page 2):

When **are** we **going**?

We **are going** soon.

TRAVEL GUIDE
COME PLAY IN THE SUN!

Sight Words
Sight words are words that you see again and again when you read. This book is filled with the sight words **are**, **going**, **they**, and **play**. Look for them in the text. Check the pictures, too!

The penguins **are going** on vacation.

2

A

Top-right (page 15):

Listen to the sentences. Then choose a sight word from the box to fill in each blank.

Word Box   **are**   **going**   **they**   **play**

1 He is _____ to the beach.

2 Let's _____ in the park.

3 When will _____ be back from vacation?

4 My brothers _____ older than me.

5 I am _____ to the baseball game.

6 We _____ writing stories today.

7 She loves to _____ soccer.

8 Can _____ come with us?

Answers: 1. going 2. play 3. they 4. are 5. going 6. are 7. play 8. they

15

Bottom-left panel (page 4):

Can I **play**?

FISH SNACKS

They are going to **play** on the beach.

4

B

Bottom-right panel (page 13):

When **are** we **going** to get there?

ANTARCTIC-AIR

They are NOT sure **they are going** to come back!

13

They are sure **they are going** to have fun.

They are going to **play** in the sun.

The penguins **are going** on vacation.

They are going to **play** in the trees.

They are going to **play** in the sand.

6

C

The penguins **are going** to pack.

11

They are going to **play** on surfboards.

8

D

They are going to **play** on skis.

9

Celebrate the new sight words you learned by saying these four short cheers.

S-o-m-e! Give a yell!
What do these four letters spell?
A sight word that we all know well —
Some, some, some!

V-e-r-y! Give a yell!
What do these four letters spell?
A sight word that we all know well —
Very, very, very!

G-o-o-d! Give a yell!
What do these four letters spell?
A sight word that we all know well —
Good, good, good!

B-u-t! Give a yell!
What do these three letters spell?
A sight word that we all know well —
But, but, but!

16

Some Dogs Are Very Good

by Mickey Daniels
illustrated by Richard Torrey

SCHOLASTIC

Sight Word Review

some	very
good	but

Do you know the four sight words in this book? Read aloud the word on each flower.

good   some

some   but   very

very   good   but

14

Roll over, Spot.

Some tricks are **very** hard.

But not Spot.

3

Roll over, Bingo. Very good!

Sight Words

Sight words are words that you see again and again when you read. This book is filled with the sight words **some**, **very**, **good**, and **but**. Look for them in the text. Check the pictures, too!

Some dogs are **very good** at doing tricks.

2

A

Sight Word Fill-ins

Listen to the sentences. Then choose a sight word from the box to fill in each blank.

Word Box	some	very	good	but

1 This soap smells _____.

2 Try _____ of this pie.

3 That dog is _____ cute.

4 She likes snakes, _____ he does not.

5 May I borrow _____ of your paper?

6 He is _____ at spelling.

7 Everyone went outside _____ me.

8 This box is _____ big.

Doggy Treats

Answers: 1. good 2. some 3. very 4. but 5. some 6. good 7. but 8. very

15

Good dog, Scooter!

Some dogs are **very good** at fetching sticks.

4

B

Good dog, Spot! Good dog!

But that is **good** enough for me!

13

Spot is **very good** at being Spot.

But not Spot.

Some dogs are **very good**—
as **good** as **good** can be.

But not Spot.

Some dogs are **very good** at staying clean and neat.

6

But not Spot.

11

Some dogs are **very good** at waiting for a treat.

8

But not Spot.

9

Sight Word Cheers

Celebrate the new sight words you learned by saying these four short cheers.

H-a-v-e! Give a yell!
What do these four letters spell?
A sight word that we all know well —
Have, have, have!

Y-o-u! Give a yell!
What do these three letters spell?
A sight word that we all know well —
You, you, you!

A-s-k! Give a yell!
What do these three letters spell?
A sight word that we all know well —
Ask, ask, ask!

H-e-r! Give a yell!
What do these three letters spell?
A sight word that we all know well —
Her, her, her!

16

Sight Word Review

Do you know the four sight words in this book? Read aloud the word on each teacup.

have
you
her
ask

ask
her
have
you

14

Sight Word Tales

Have You Seen Jellybean?

by Maria Fleming
illustrated by Amy Wummer

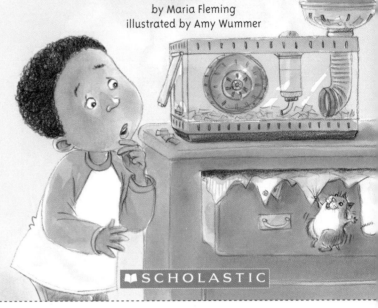

SCHOLASTIC

Have you seen **her**?

I **ask** my brother, "**Have you** seen Jellybean?"
"I **have** not seen **her**," my brother says.

3

Left page (book pages)

Where are **you**, Jellybean?

Sight Words

Sight words are words that you see again and again when you read. This book is filled with the sight words **have**, **you**, **ask**, and **her**. Look for them in the text. Check the pictures, too!

My hamster, Jellybean, got out of **her** cage. I **have** to find **her**!

2

A

Have you seen **her**?

I **ask** my sister, "**Have you** seen Jellybean?" "I **have** not seen **her**," my sister says.

4

B

Right page

Sight Word Fill-ins

Listen to the sentences. Then choose a sight word from the box to fill in each blank.

Word Box	have	you	ask	her

1 She lost _____ mitten.

2 May I _____ some popcorn?

3 Do _____ walk to school?

4 They _____ us for help.

5 This is _____ favorite book.

6 Can _____ come over today?

7 We _____ two cats.

8 I _____ the teacher a question.

Answers: 1. her 2. have 3. you 4. ask 5. her 6. you 7. have 8. ask

15

She closes **her** eyes. Good night, Jellybean. I hope **you have** dreams as sweet as **you**!

13

I put Jellybean in **her** cage.
"**You have** to rest now," I tell **her**.

12

I **ask** my mother, "**Have you** seen
Jellybean?"
"I **have** not seen **her**," my mother says.

5

Jellybean! I **have** found **you** at last!

10

I **ask** my friend, "**Have you** seen Jellybean?"
"I **have** not seen **her**," my friend says.

7

I **ask** my father, "**Have you** seen Jellybean?"
"I **have** not seen **her**," my father says.

6   C

I **ask her**, "Where **have you** been hiding?"
Jellybean just wiggles **her** whiskers.

11

I **ask** my neighbor, "**Have you** seen
Jellybean?"
"I **have** not seen **her**," my neighbor says.

8   D

Oh, Jellybean! Where **have you** gone?
I miss **you** so much!

9

Sight Word Cheers

Celebrate the new sight words you learned by saying these four short cheers.

H-e-l-p! Give a yell!
What do these four letters spell?
A sight word that we all know well —
Help, help, help!

T-h-e-m! Give a yell!
What do these four letters spell?
A sight word that we all know well —
Them, them, them!

A-l-l! Give a yell!
What do these three letters spell?
A sight word that we all know well —
All, all, all!

J-u-s-t! Give a yell!
What do these four letters spell?
A sight word that we all know well —
Just, just, just!

16

Sight Word Tales

All Puffins Just Love Muffins

by Jane Quinn
illustrated by Bill Dare

SCHOLASTIC

Sight Word Review

Do you know the four sight words in this book? Read aloud the word on each muffin.

them   just

help   all   help

all   them   just

14

Sure. I will **help** you **all**.

Please help us make muffins!

Just Muffins

They need somebody, maybe you,
to **help them** bake a batch or two.

3

Just look at **all** the hungry puffins —
dreaming **all** day long of muffins.

A

Sight Words

Sight words are words that you see
again and again when you read. This
book is filled with the sight words **help**,
them, **all**, and **just**. Look for them in
the text. Check the pictures, too!

Sight Word Fill-ins

help them
all just

**Listen to the sentences. Then choose a sight
word from the box to fill in each blank.**

Word Box	help	them	all	just

1 I can _____ you tie your shoes.

2 She _____ loves that movie!

3 Where did you put _____?

4 We gave _____ of the puppies away.

5 He likes to _____ his mom rake leaves.

6 I had _____ one cookie.

7 Their teacher took _____ to the museum.

8 Where did _____ of the ducks go?

Answers: 1. help 2. just 3. them 4. all 5. help 6. just 7. them 8. all

---

All of **them**
look good, but
let's **just** make
the blueberry.

Just Muffins

Help them choose a recipe.
All puffins **just** love muffins!

B

Just one left?
All for me?
Thank you!

Because. . .
all puffins **just** love muffins!

Time for **them** to EAT THE MUFFINS!
And, as you can tell,
all the puffins do this well.

Help **them** measure carefully.
All puffins **just** love muffins!

Just one more thing for **them** to do —

Help **them** add the flour, too.
All puffins **just** love muffins!

Help them add the eggs — **just** a few.
All puffins **just** love muffins!

6

C

all by themselves, no **help** from you. . .

11

Help them mix the berries in.
All puffins **just** love muffins!

8

D

Help them fill each muffin tin.
All puffins **just** love muffins!

9

Celebrate the new sight words you learned by saying these four short cheers.

T-o-d-a-y! Give a yell!
What do these five letters spell?
A sight word that we all know well —
Today, today, today!

S-o! Give a yell!
What do these two letters spell?
A sight word that we all know well —
So, so, so!

A-s! Give a yell!
What do these two letters spell?
A sight word that we all know well —
As, as, as!

W-e-l-l! Give a yell!
What do these four letters spell?
A sight word that we all know well —
Well, well, well!

16

Today Is So Boring!

by Catherine Bittner
illustrated by Doug Jones

SCHOLASTIC

Do you know the four sight words in this book? Read aloud the word on each bubble.

today
as
well
so
well
so
as
today

14

It's **so** dull **today**. It's **so** totally boring.
I might **as well** be snoozing and snoring.

3

Oh, **today** is **as** boring **as** boring can be.
There's nothing **today** to do or see.

A

Sight Word Fill-ins

today so
as well

Listen to the sentences. Then choose a sight word from the box to fill in each blank.

Word Box	today	so	as	well

1. That puppy is _____ cute!
2. They went to the park _____.
3. She dressed up _____ a fairy for the play.
4. Will _____ be hot or cold?
5. Our teacher is not feeling _____.
6. We worked _____ a team on the project.
7. I am _____ happy to see you!
8. He plays the piano very _____.

Answers: 1. so 2. today 3. as 4. today 5. well 6. as 7. so 8. well

I might **as well** just stare at the sky.
I might **as well** watch the clouds drift by.

B

I might **as well** snooze. I might **as well** snore.
I just hope tomorrow won't be such a bore!

I might **as well** go to bed early **today**.
Oh, **today** was **so** boring in every way.

Today is **so** boring.
I just feel like snoring.

I am **so** bored **today**.

I might **as well** just stare at the clock.
I might **as well** count each tick and tock.

Today is **so** boring.
I just feel like snoring.

I might **as well** count each blade of grass.
I might **as well** count the ants **as** they pass.

C

Today is **so** boring.
I just feel like snoring.

I might **as well** watch a dull TV show.
I might **as well** watch my fingernails grow.

D

Today is **so** boring.
I just feel like snoring.

Sight Word Cheers

Celebrate the new sight words you learned by saying these four short cheers.

M-a-n-y! Give a yell!
What do these four letters spell?
A sight word that we all know well —
Many, many, many!

W-h-i-c-h! Give a yell!
What do these five letters spell?
A sight word that we all know well —
Which, which, which!

K-i-n-d! Give a yell!
What do these four letters spell?
A sight word that we all know well —
Kind, kind, kind!

B-u-y! Give a yell!
What do these three letters spell?
A sight word that we all know well —
Buy, buy, buy!

16

Sight Word Review

Do you know the four sight words in this book? Read aloud the word on each shoe.

many

buy

many   kind   which

which   buy   kind

14

Sight Word Tales

So Many Kinds of Shoes!

by Maria Fleming
illustrated by Beccy Blake

SCHOLASTIC

Maybe I will **buy** this **kind**.

Will she **buy** the **kind** for running races?

3

So **many** different **kinds**!

Best Buy in Town!

Buy One, Get One Free

Sight Words Fact

Sight words are words that you see again and again when you read. This book is filled with the sight words **many**, **kind**, **which**, and **buy**. Look for them in the text. Check the pictures, too!

Spider needs to **buy** new shoes.
Which kind of shoes will Spider choose?

2

A

Sight Word Fill-ins

Listen to the sentences. Then choose a sight word from the box to fill in each blank.

Word Box	**many**	**which**	**kind**	**buy**

1 He has _____ friends.

2 Tell me _____ one you want.

3 What _____ of dog is that?

4 We went to the store to _____ milk.

5 How _____ pennies are in the jar?

6 Vanilla is her favorite _____ of ice cream.

7 He will _____ new sneakers today.

8 I don't know _____ way to go.

Answers: 1. many 2. which 3. kind 4. buy 5. many 6. kind 7. buy 8. which

15

Or maybe I will **buy** this **kind**.

Will she **buy** the **kind** with purple laces?

4

B

With so **many** feet, I could **buy** every **kind**!

Spider has made up her mind.
She **buys** one of every **kind**!

13

I have **many** feet!

Many shoes, but **many** feet.
Many feet just can't be beat!

12

I like this **kind**, too!
Which kind should
I **buy**?

So **many** different **kinds** of shoes!
Which kind of shoes will Spider choose?

5

This **kind** of shoe
is fancy!

Will she **buy** the **kind** with flowered straps?

10

This **kind** would
come in handy.

Will she **buy** the **kind** for a rainy day?

7

Will she **buy** the **kind** to dance ballet?

C

So **many** different **kinds** of shoes!
Which kind of shoes will Spider choose?

So **many** different **kinds** of shoes!
Which kind of shoes will Spider choose?

D

Will she **buy** the **kind** with noisy taps?

Sight Word Cheers

Celebrate the new sight words you learned by saying these four short cheers.

W-h-o! Give a yell!
What do these three letters spell?
A sight word that we all know well —
Who, who, who!

W-o-u-l-d! Give a yell!
What do these five letters spell?
A sight word that we all know well —
Would, would, would!

T-h-e-s-e! Give a yell!
What do these five letters spell?
A sight word that we all know well —
These, these, these!

F-u-n-n-y! Give a yell!
What do these five letters spell?
A sight word that we all know well —
Funny, funny, funny!

16

Sight Word Review

Do you know the four sight words in this book? Read aloud the word on each hat.

14

Who Would Buy These Clothes?

by Catherine Bittner
illustrated by Richard Torrey

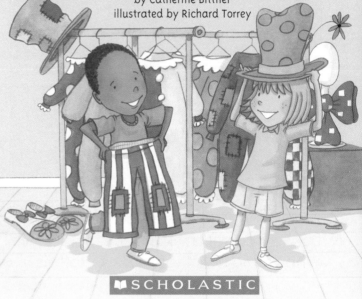

SCHOLASTIC

Look at **these funny** pants!

Who would buy **these funny** pants?

3

Sight Words

Sight words are words that you see again and again when you read. This book is filled with the sight words **who**, **would**, **these**, and **funny**. Look for them in the text. Check the pictures, too!

Look at **these**! Look at those!
Who would buy **these funny** clothes?

2

A

Sight Word Fill-ins

who would these funny

Listen to the sentences. Then choose a sight word from the box to fill in each blank.

Word Box   **who   would   these   funny**

1 We read a _____ book.

2 I think _____ flowers smell good.

3 Do you know _____ drew this picture?

4 They _____ not go home.

5 That joke was very _____.

6 Where should I put _____?

7 Guess _____ won the prize!

8 She _____ like to come with us.

Answers: 1. funny 2. these 3. who 4. would 5. funny 6. these 7. who 8. would

15

Who would buy **these funny** shirts?

4

B

clowns!

13

Oh! That's **who would** buy **these funny** clothes. . .

Who would buy **these funny** ties?

Who would buy **these funny** wigs?

Who would buy **these funny** shoes?
Who would buy **these funny** boots?

Who would buy **these funny** skirts?

Who would buy **these funny** gowns?

Who would buy **these funny** hats?

Who would buy **these funny** suits?

Sight Word Cheers

Celebrate the new sight words you learned by saying these four short cheers.

T-r-y! Give a yell!
What do these three letters spell?
A sight word that we all know well —
Try, try, try!

A-g-a-i-n! Give a yell!
What do these five letters spell?
A sight word that we all know well —
Again, again, again!

F-a-l-l! Give a yell!
What do these four letters spell?
A sight word that we all know well —
Fall, fall, fall!

D-o-w-n! Give a yell!
What do these four letters spell?
A sight word that we all know well —
Down, down, down!

16

Sight Word Tales

Try Again, Hen!

by Jane Quinn
illustrated by Franfou

SCHOLASTIC

Sight Word Review

Do you know the four sight words in this book? Read aloud the word on each skateboard.

again

try

fall

down

try

again

down

fall

14

I will give it a **try**. I hope I don't **fall**.

"I hope I don't **fall**," says Hen.
She hops on and rolls **down** the road.

3

Sight Words

Sight words are words that you see again and again when you read. This book is filled with the sight words **try**, **again**, **fall**, and **down**. Look for them in the text. Check the pictures, too!

Hen has a new skateboard. She wants to **try** to ride it.

2

A

Whoops!
Try again, Hen!

SLOP! Hen **falls** in the mud.
"**Try again**, Hen!" says Pig.

4

B

try   again
fall   down

Sight Word Fill-ins

Listen to the sentences. Then choose a sight word from the box to fill in each blank.

Word Box	**try**	**again**	**fall**	**down**

1. I will _____ to hit the ball.

2. May we go to the museum _____?

3. The leaves _____ off the trees in autumn.

4. They rode their bikes _____ the hill.

5. She will _____ to spell the word.

6. The cat climbed _____ the stairs.

7. I want to see that movie _____!

8. We watched snow _____ from the sky.

Answers: 1. try 2. again 3. fall 4. down 5. try 6. down 7. again 8. fall

15

Here I go!
I hope I don't
fall down!

"Of course you may **try**," says Hen.
And they do—**again** and **again** and **again**!

13

If at first you don't succeed, **try**, **try again**!

I really want to **try**, too!

Wow! I want to **try**!

"May we **try** to ride your skateboard?" Pig, Sheep, and Duck ask Hen.

I will **try** not to **fall down again**.

Hen rolls **down** the road **again**.

This is fun! Wheeeee!

Hen does not **fall** in the mud. She does not **fall** in the hay. She does not **fall** in the pond.

I will **try** not to **fall down again**.

Hen rolls **down** the road **again**.

FLOP! Hen **falls** in the hay.
"**Try again**, Hen!" says Sheep.

6

Hen does not **fall** at all!
"Hooray for Hen!" the animals shout.

11

PLOP! Hen **falls** in the pond.
"**Try again**, Hen!" says Duck.

8

Hen rolls **down** the road **again**. **Down, down, down** she rolls.

9

Celebrate the new sight words you learned by saying these four short cheers.

T-a-k-e! Give a yell!
What do these four letters spell?
A sight word that we all know well —
Take, take, take!

T-o-g-e-t-h-e-r! Give a yell!
What do these eight letters spell?
A sight word that we all know well —
Together, together, together!

T-h-e-n! Give a yell!
What do these four letters spell?
A sight word that we all know well —
Then, then, then!

A-r-o-u-n-d! Give a yell!
What do these six letters spell?
A sight word that we all know well —
Around, around, around!

16

Let's Make Soup Together

by Mickey Daniels
illustrated by Mike Gordon

SCHOLASTIC

Do you know the four sight words in this book? Read aloud the word on each bowl.

together
take
around
then
together
take
then
around

14

Together, we'll make silly soup.
Take a look at how it's done.

3

Take a look at this recipe.

Sight Words

Sight words are words that you see again and again when you read. This book is filled with the sight words **take, together, then,** and **around**. Look for them in the text. Check the pictures, too!

Gather **around**, one and all.
Let's cook up some fun.

2

A

Sight Word Fill-ins

take together
then around

Listen to the sentences. Then choose a sight word from the box to fill in each blank.

Word Box   **take   together   then   around**

1 Put on your socks, _____ put on your shoes.

2 Let's play a game _____.

3 Will you _____ me to the park?

4 He skated _____ the rink.

5 She put a puzzle _____.

6 I brushed my teeth, _____ went to bed.

7 The squirrel ran _____ the tree.

8 We can _____ turns on the swing.

Answers: 1. then 2. together 3. take 4. around 5. together 5. then 7. around 8. take

15

Take soda pop.
Take one pork chop.
Take pickles — quite a lot.

4

B

Please **take** this bowl away!

I can't **take** another bite!

Silly soup is soup-er fun —
until you have to eat it!

13

For silly fun **together**,
no soup **around** can beat it.

Mix them all **together**,
then skip **around** the pot.

Take jellybeans.
Take tangerines.
Take mustard — quite a lot.

Mix them all **together**,
then march **around** the pot.

Take squishy peas.
Take stinky cheese.
Take oatmeal — quite a lot.

6

Mix them all **together**,
then it's time to heat the pot.

11

Take macaroni.
Take old baloney.
Take jelly — quite a lot.

8

Mix them all **together**,
then dance **around** the pot.

9

Sight Word Cheers

Celebrate the new sight words you learned by saying these four short cheers.

P-l-e-a-s-e! Give a yell!
What do these six letters spell?
A sight word that we all know well —
Please, please, please!

S-t-o-p! Give a yell!
What do these four letters spell?
A sight word that we all know well —
Stop, stop, stop!

I-f! Give a yell!
What do these two letters spell?
A sight word that we all know well —
If, if, if!

M-u-s-t! Give a yell!
What do these four letters spell?
A sight word that we all know well —
Must, must, must!

16

Sight Word Tales

Please Stop Monkeying Around!

by Maria Fleming
illustrated by Kelly Kennedy

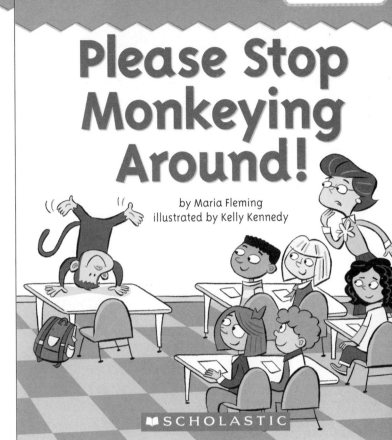

SCHOLASTIC

Sight Word Review

Do you know the four sight words in this book? Read aloud the word on each hat.

stop   please

please   must   if

if   stop   must

14

But **if** you stay, you **must** behave.
Please, Monkey, do your best.

3

Class Rules

You **must** be polite.
You **must** listen to others.
You **must** talk quietly.
You **must** raise your hand.

Please come in!

Welcome, Monkey! **Please** come in.
We're glad that you're our guest.

2

A

Sight Word Fill-ins

please if
stop must

Listen to the sentences. Then choose a sight word from the box to fill in each blank.

Word Box	please	stop	if	must

1 He _____ be very tired.

2 Ask your mom _____ you can come.

3 You _____ finish your work.

4 They will _____ by to visit.

5 Will you _____ talk quietly!

6 I can watch TV _____ I clean my room.

7 She had to _____ playing and go home.

8 May I _____ stay up late?

Answers: 1. must 2. if 3. must 4. stop 5. please 6. if 7. stop 8. please

15

You **must stop** that!

Please stop hanging upside down.
Please stop swinging to and fro.

4

B

Please don't visit us again.
We would rather visit you!

13

If you **must** monkey around,
you **must** do so at the zoo.

Please stop monkeying around!
If you don't, then you **must** go.

Please stop snacking on bananas.
Please stop breaking every rule.

Please stop monkeying around!
If you don't, then you **must** go.

Please stop writing on the wall.
Please stop playing tic-tac-toe.

6

C

Please start packing up your things.
You **must** go. **Please** leave our school!

Please stop dancing on the desk.
Please stop putting on a show.

8

D

Please stop monkeying around!
If you don't, then you **must** go.

9

Sight Word Cheers

Celebrate the new sight words you learned by saying these four short cheers.

L-i-t-t-l-e! Give a yell!
What do these six letters spell?
A sight word that we all know well —
Little, little, little!

H-a-s! Give a yell!
What do these three letters spell?
A sight word that we all know well —
Has, has, has!

F-i-n-d! Give a yell!
What do these four letters spell?
A sight word that we all know well —
Find, find, find!

F-o-u-n-d! Give a yell!
What do these five letters spell?
A sight word that we all know well —
Found, found, found!

16

Sight Word Tales

Little Bo-Peep's Lost-and-Found Sheep

by Jane Quinn
illustrated by Kelly Kennedy

SCHOLASTIC

Sight Word Review

Do you know the four sight words in this book? Read aloud the word on each sheep.

find   found

little   has   find

has   found   little

14

I **found** one!

The spoon **has** run off without me!

She **finds** one with a spoon on the run.

3

I must find those naughty little sheep!

Sight Words

Sight words are words that you see again and again when you read. This book is filled with the sight words **little**, **has**, **find**, and **found**. Look for them in the text. Check the pictures, too!

Little Bo-Peep **has** lost 15 sheep.
Poor **little** lass! She must **find** them all fast!

2

A

Sight Word Fill-ins

little   has
find   found

Listen to the sentences. Then choose a sight word from the box to fill in each blank.

Word Box   little   has   find   found

1. My sister _____ not come home yet.
2. Ladybugs are very _____.
3. They cannot _____ their mittens.
4. He _____ five dollars on the ground.
5. May I have a _____ more milk?
6. She _____ blue eyes.
7. Last week, we _____ a frog in the woods.
8. Where did you _____ that book?

Answers: 1. has 2. little 3. find 4. found 5. little 6. has 7. found 8. find

15

I found two more!

Look! It's Little Bo-Peep! She has found her sheep.

She **finds** two in a very big shoe.

4

B

She found us, but we can't find her!

Now all of the sheep must **find Little** Bo-Peep!

13

The **little** lass sneaks away
to hide in some hay.

Little Bo-Peep **has found** three of her sheep!
But the **little** lass must **find** the rest fast.

She **finds** three more doing a chore.

Little Bo-Peep **has found** nine of her sheep!
But the **little** lass must **find** the rest fast.

She **finds** six on a wall made of bricks.

6

C

Little Bo-Peep **has found** all 15 sheep!
She **has found** every one!
Time for a **little** fun.

11

She **finds** three in a tub on the sea.

8

D

Little Bo-Peep **has found** 12 of her sheep!
But the **little** lass must **find** the rest fast.

9

Celebrate the new sight words you learned by saying these four short cheers.

O-n-c-e! Give a yell!
What do these four letters spell?
A sight word that we all know well —
Once, once, once!

U-p-o-n! Give a yell!
What do these four letters spell?
A sight word that we all know well —
Upon, upon, upon!

F-a-r! Give a yell!
What do these three letters spell?
A sight word that we all know well —
Far, far, far!

A-w-a-y! Give a yell!
What do these four letters spell?
A sight word that we all know well —
Away, away, away!

16

Once Upon a Planet

by Mickey Daniels
illustrated by Doug Jones

SCHOLASTIC

Sight Word Review

once upon far away

Do you know the four sight words in this book? Read aloud the word on each star.

upon   far   once   upon

once   away   far   away

14

Maybe I will find a friend somewhere **far, far away**.

At least **once** a week, he flew **far away** hoping to come **upon** a friend one day.

3

It is lonely upon this planet.

Sight Words

Sight words are words that you see again and again when you read. This book is filled with the sight words **once, upon, far,** and **away**. Look for them in the text. Check the pictures, too!

Once upon a planet, near the galaxy's end, one lonely alien longed for a friend.

2

A

Sight Word Fill-ins

once upon far away

Listen to the sentences. Then choose a sight word from the box to fill in each blank.

Word Box	once	upon	far	away

1. The frog sat _____ the lily pad.
2. Please put _____ your crayons.
3. How _____ can you run?
4. The cat climbed _____ my lap.
5. Please come here at _____ !
6. We rode our bikes very _____ today.
7. He threw _____ his broken toys.
8. They all yelled "Surprise!" at _____.

Answers: 1. upon 2. away 3. far 4. upon 5. once 6. far 7. away 8. once

15

It is lonely upon this planet.

Once upon a planet, **far, far away,** another alien played alone every day.

4

B

Okay! Let's race once around the galaxy!

two lonely aliens each found a friend!

13

Once upon a planet, near the galaxy's end,

At least **once** a week, he flew **far away** hoping to come **upon** a friend one day.

And **upon** that planet, **far away** from the sun,

They both wished for a friend,
who wanted to play
upon planets near and **far, far away**.

Once **upon** two planets, **away** so **far**, the two wished **upon** the very same star.

C

those aliens met and had tons of fun!

Then, **once upon** a planet, **far, far away,**

both aliens landed the very same day.

D

Sight Word Tales Teaching Guide